"Letters to Myself"
(Parables of Sakura)

Nina Kasáne

2025

ISBN: 979-8-9990362-2-3

© 2025 Nina Kasáne

All rights reserved

No part of this book may be reproduced, stored in a retrieval system, or transmitted in any form or by any means – electronic, mechanical, photocopying, recording, or otherwise – without the prior written permission of the author.

First edition.

Self-published in Orlando, Florida.

Printed in the United States of America.

Before you open this book

Let me be completely honest with you on these pages.
And with myself, too.

This isn't just a book. These are letters.
The kind we never send to anyone.
Letters that stay tucked away in drawers or memories.
The ones that hurt – and heal.

Everything here is real: the shame and the strength.
The exhaustion no one sees.
The dreams we hid in old shoeboxes.
The words that never made it past our lips –
but were preserved in silence.

This is a book for those who know how to listen to themselves.
And for those who are just learning.

I won't give you answers.
I'll just stay close.
Maybe you will recognize yourself.

Maybe you will remember who you were –
before you began to hide.

Because these letters are for you.
But most of all – they're to me.

With gentleness and quiet,
Nina Kasáne

Table of Contents

Chapter 0. The Parable of the Girl and the Book of Her Life 8
Chapter 1. The Ink of the Heart 10
Chapter 2. The Light That Remains 12
Chapter 3. Where Miracles Are Born 15
Chapter 4. The Tree That Never Bloomed 19
Chapter 5. Stones That Never Became a Road 23
Chapter 6. Paths That No Longer Walk Together 26
Chapter 7. The City of Handcrafted Bridges 28
Chapter 9. The One They Forgot 36
Chapter 10. The One Who Waited for Her Father 39
Chapter 11. Rainbow Leggings 42
Chapter 12. The Jacket the Color of Childhood 45
Chapter 13. The Cake 48
Chapter 14. Where the Stage Begins with the Heart 51
Chapter 15. The Pink Cat 54
Chapter 16. The Story That Never Existed .,,,,,.................................... 57
Chapter 17. Health to Your Hands 60
Chapter 18. A Samurai Has No Goal, Only a Path 63
Chapter 19. The One Who Showed Not a Map, but the Road 66
Chapter 20. As Long as Her Voice Sings 68
Chapter 21. The One Who Lives Under the Couch 71
Chapter 22. Once – and Never Again 74
Chapter 23. The Bird 76
Chapter 24. Ashen Light 79
Chapter 25. Where the Wind Begins 81

Chapter 26. The Queen's Gambit 84
Chapter 27. Paper Birds 87
Chapter 28. All Roads – A Web Leading to Yourself 90
Chapter 29. Where Every Step Echoes 94
Chapter 30. The Room Where Words Wait 98
Chapter 31. The Station of Unsubmitted Trains 103
Chapter 32. One Day, the House Fell Silent 107
Chapter 33. The Mirror of the Edge: Before You Disappear 114
Chapter 34. Crystal Deserts 118
Chapter 35. The Flower Passage 121
Chapter 36. How Much of You Remains 125
Chapter 37. A Time Capsule: From the Future – to Childhood 128
Chapter 38. A Word You Can Say Only Once 131
Chapter 39. The True Cost of a Ticket 134
Chapter 40. A Mirror Without Reflection 139
Chapter 41. The Home That Lives Inside 143
Chapter 42. The One Who Doesn't Catch the Ball 146
Chapter 43. The Ascendant: The Mirror of Aries 150
Chapter 44. A Classmate 153
Chapter 45. Between the Brush and the Heart 155
Chapter 46. The Distant Voice 158
Chapter 47. A Dream on a Nail Behind the Door 162
Chapter 48. The Mist No One Saw 165
Chapter 49. The Diary of Memory 169
Chapter 50. The Circle of Air 172
Chapter 51. A Dress to Grow Into 177
Chapter 52. The Valley of Unsent Signs 179
Chapter 53. When Love Suffocates 183

Chapter 54. The Stone No One Stepped On 185
Chapter 55. The Path of the White Wind 187
Chapter 56. The Parable of the Comet and the Cornfield 189
Chapter 57. The Girl Who Followed the Sound of Music 193
Chapter 58. Sakura and the Strawberry 195
Chapter 59. When Love is Wrapped in a Gift 198
Chapter 60. An Envelope with a Personal Meaning 203
Chapter 61. When Someone Sees More Than Just the Crowd 209
Chapter 62. When Strict Eyes Hide Quiet Support 212
Chapter 63. When Pain Teaches Us to Love Even More 219
Chapter 64. When the Silence of the Stage Becomes Yours 223
Chapter 65. The Star at the Desk 228
Chapter 67. The Only Ice 238
Chapter 68. The Radio-tower and the Stars 244
Chapter 69. When Friendship Was a Spell 249
Chapter 70. When Your Place is Taken 255
Chapter 71. Those Who Travel Light Are the Ones Who Stay 259
Chapter 72. The Color of a Mistake 267
Chapter 73. 故郷 – furusato – The Homeland of the Soul 271
Chapter 74. When the Heart Learns to Wait 275
Chapter 75. When the World Spoke with Her Voice 282
Chapter 76. Epilogue: A Letter to Myself 289

Chapter 0. The Parable of the Girl and the Book of Her Life

Once, there lived a girl named Sakura.
She was quiet, observant, and a little melancholic. From an early age, Sakura knew what it meant to feel alone. When her parents separated, an emptiness settled in her small heart. And yet, in that moment, she made herself a promise: one day, she would create a family filled with love, care, and warmth.
Years passed. Sakura moved from place to place, learned new languages, adapted to unfamiliar rules and customs. Her life was full of twists – unexpected, difficult, and sometimes miraculous. She tried her hand at different things, searching for what stirred her soul, and each time she began again from scratch. There were disappointments, but also victories.

Sometimes, she felt lost – as if she'd strayed from the path. But inside her, a quiet flame kept burning: "I will get through this."

One especially difficult evening, when everything seemed to be falling apart, Sakura found herself alone in the silence. She lowered her gaze – and saw a large, beautiful book resting on her knees. On its cover were the words:
"The Book of Your Life."

She opened it – and saw her past: the joy and the pain, all that she had endured. On its pages were moments of strength, fear, tears, embraces, laughter, and silence. Everything she thought was long forgotten had been kept.

And then – a blank page.

"Why is it empty?" Sakura whispered.

And a voice answered – not from outside, but from deep within:

"Because you are still breathing. And that means you can still change everything.
Each day is a new chapter.
You are the author. And you have the right to begin again."

Sakura closed the book and pressed it tightly to her chest.
From that moment on, she no longer feared the empty pages.

She knew as long as her heart was beating, she had the chance to write her story anew.
And she would write it with love.

You are not merely the author of your story.
You are its breath, its voice, its light.
A story is not built from perfect days –
But from true ones.

Yours,
Sakura

Chapter 1. The Ink of the Heart

After the night Sakura first saw her Book of Life, many things changed – not in the world around her, but within.

Now she woke with a different feeling.
Not because life had become easier, but because she knew: each morning was a chance to write something real.

The book no longer lived only in her imagination. She could almost feel its weight – in her hands, in her choices, in her words.
And day by day, the pages filled with living moments:
– The day she watched her daughter laughing with friends and thought: "This is joy, right here."
– The morning her son pressed his cheek to hers and said, "Mom, it's always good with you."
– The evening the whole family lay close together, in silence, wrapped in warmth.

Sakura realized: the book is not filled with events, but with feelings.
Dates don't matter – gazes do.
Headlines aren't needed – only embraces.

She wrote – not with a pen, but with her heart. And even on the hardest days, when her body was tired and her thoughts were heavy, she

would write:
"Today, I didn't give up. Today, I chose love."

Her son became her strength. His kindness – a reminder that love lives in every word.
Her daughter – her inspiration, proof of how beautiful the voice of the future can sound.
And her family – her quiet harbor, where she could be herself without fear.

As long as laughter echoes in your home,
As long as you hold your loved ones close,
As long as you love –
Your book is alive.

Yours,
Sakura

Chapter 2. The Light That Remains
Time had passed.
Sakura no longer searched for reasons to start over–
she simply lived.

With gratitude.
With quietness within.
With tenderness in every movement.

Sometimes, she would sit on the porch with a cup of tea and watch the sunlight kiss her son's face.
Hear her daughter laugh as if the world held no heavy shadows.
And in those moments, Sakura knew–this was a miracle.
Not loud.
Not dazzling.
But alive.

She felt that a second chance was not some gift to leave forgotten on a shelf.
It was breath.
It was a glance.
It was the chance to say "I love you"–even if yesterday she'd remained silent.
It was the chance to forgive.
Herself.
The world.
Life.

And in Sakura's heart there was silence—
the kind God leaves behind after performing a
miracle in the place of loss.
Not to restore what once was,
but to create something different.
Deeper.
Brighter.
True.

Sometimes, her daughter would pick up a
notebook and start to draw.
Sometimes, someone close would say:
"When you're near, I believe everything is still
possible."
And then Sakura understood—
her book had come alive not only for her.

She didn't teach.
Didn't persuade.
Didn't prove anything.
She simply lived.
With love.
And God—the One who once placed a blank page
into her hands—
was now writing through her in the books of
others.

Softly.
Gently.
With light.

Sometimes, a second chance is a gift wrapped in tears.
Sometimes, the miracle is not that everything goes back to how it was,
but that you're still here.

Yours,
Sakura

Chapter 3. Where Miracles Are Born

It happened at the end of summer.
The sun had begun to set more quietly,
and the wind, as if sensing what was to come,
carried a hushed warning.
Sakura loved this time of year –
it always brought her silence.
But that year, the silence was different –
deep, taut,
like the hush before a storm.

One day, their family was swept into the heart of pain.
What once felt solid
suddenly cracked.
The body – broken.
The heart – afraid.
Life – turned upside down.

Their little boy could no longer stand.
The prognosis – unclear.
Words – cautious.
The future – veiled in mist.

And yet, in that silence, one thread remained: faith.
Not the kind that shouts.
The kind that holds,
even when everything trembles.

Sakura herself was weak.
She could not reach out.
She could not rise.
But her love spoke without words.
She was simply there.
Even in stillness – she gave support.

And the boy...
He began his journey.
Not a heroic one.
Each step – through pain.
Tears.
Crying.
Sometimes – screams.
His legs failed him.
But something within refused to surrender.
There was a thirst for life inside him.
And beside him – those who believed,
when he could not.

He walked.
And one day –
he walked on his own.
It was more than a step.
It was a miracle,
born of love,
and pain,
and a silence that never gave up.

His sister changed, too.
Gentle, radiant –
she became stronger.
One day, she said:

"It's okay to be weak, Mama. I'm here now."
And Sakura saw –
her little girl had grown.
Not outwardly,
but deep within.

Her husband grew quieter.
But in that quiet – he held the home together.
He didn't demand.
He didn't complain.
He simply was –
and that was enough.

Time passed.
Her son ran again.
Her daughter glowed from within.
And Sakura, sitting in the shade of a tree,
watched them and thought:
sometimes a miracle is not what arrives.
But what remains.

And if you are walking through darkness now –
know this:
you are not alone.
The miracle is already with you.

Just walk.
As far as you can.
And if you cannot walk –
then lie down with faith.
That, too, is a kind of movement.

With you always,
Sakura

Chapter 4. The Tree That Never Bloomed

One cool evening, Sakura walked toward the edge of the village.
There, she saw an elderly woman sitting on a bench,
watering a tree that looked lifeless.
It hadn't bloomed in years.

Sakura approached and gently asked:
– "Forgive me, but why do you keep doing this? It doesn't seem to come back to life…"

The woman looked at her and replied:
– "I planted this tree when I was dreaming of a different life.
Back then, I thought everything would follow a plan:
a good job, travels, meaningful work.
I cared for this tree as I cared for that dream."

– "But one day, a storm came.
It broke the trunk.
Everything changed.
Life went in a direction I never imagined..."

– "And still... you return?"

– "Yes.
At first, I was angry.
Then I grieved.
I wanted to forget.
But in time, I understood –
just because a dream didn't come true
doesn't mean it was meaningless.
It guided me.
It gave me strength.
And even though this tree no longer blooms,
it's still a part of me.

I don't water it for the fruit.
I water it to remember how deeply I once
believed –
to keep my heart from freezing over."

Sakura was silent for a long time.
Her heart stirred.
She too knew what it meant
to build a path,
to study,
to dream –
only to see everything collapse.
To stand in the ruins
not knowing where to go.
Feeling utterly alone.

The woman looked at her kindly.
– "Don't burn your past just because it didn't
become your future.
Sometimes, something new grows from the
ashes.
You just don't know what it is yet."

Sakura walked to the well and brought back
water.
She didn't know if anything would grow –

but she suddenly realized:
she was ready to try.

Sometimes life shatters our plans without warning.
We lose our dreams, our direction –
and it feels like we've lost ourselves.
But even if the path ends, you are not lost.
Everything you gave –
your effort, your faith, your love –
it is part of you still.
Allow yourself to grieve…
and then,
learn to love something new.
Even if it wasn't in your plans.

With you always,
Sakura

Chapter 5. Stones That Never Became a Road

Sakura walked along the riverbank,
a quiet place rarely visited.
There, by a fire, sat a master.
Around him lay a mandala of stones –
carefully arranged,
but with a hollow space in the center.

– "What is this circle?" she asked.

– "This is the Mandala of Missed Chances," he answered.
"I come here when I meet those who are afraid to walk forward.
Afraid to fail.
To be imperfect.
To start again.
Or simply to hear their own voice."

He picked up a stone from the ground.
– "This one – a girl who dreamed of painting, but never opened a single color."

– "This – a boy who was scared to look foolish, so he never said yes to his dream."

– "And this one…"
He looked away.
– "This one's mine.
Once, I chose silence over action.
I waited for the 'perfect time.'"

Sakura fell quiet.
She remembered the times she too had postponed
what called to her.
Told herself: "Later. When I'm ready.
When I'm sure."
But later never came.

– "Why is the center empty?" she asked.

– "Because only the one who dares to take a step
can place a stone there.
Not as a memory of fear,
but as a sign they moved through it.
Only then does the mandala come to life."

The master handed Sakura a smooth stone.
She held it in her palm.
It was more than a stone –
it was her "What if I fail?"
her "I'm not good enough, there are others

better,"
her "This dream isn't meant for me,"
"They'll never choose me... I won't make it."

Sakura stepped forward
and slowly placed the stone in the center.

At that moment,
the clouds parted –
and sunlight touched the mandala.
It began to glow from within.

Many paths were never taken –
not because they didn't exist,
but because someone didn't believe they were worthy.
Dreams don't demand perfection –
they only ask for a step.

With you always,
Sakura

Chapter 6. Paths That No Longer Walk Together

Sakura walked along the forest path with her friend. They had been together for so long.
Laughed together as they walked in the rain.
Shared an apple. Talked through the night by the campfire.
Sometimes, they simply stayed silent – and that was enough.
It was that rare kind of "together" that felt like forever.

Sakura remembered how once they had both been lost – and found their way only because they held each other's hand.
"I wouldn't have made it without you," she thought.

But with each new turn in the path, something began to change.
Her friend paused more often, gazed off in another direction, started conversations where Sakura no longer recognized herself.
And one day, the road split.
Her friend walked confidently down one trail.
Sakura felt another calling her.

They stood at the crossroads.

– "But we were walking together," Sakura whispered.

Her friend nodded, a gentle, wistful smile on her lips:
– "Yes. And I am grateful for every step. But now, my path calls me there."

Sakura felt everything inside her tighten. Her heart wanted to run after her.
But her soul whispered quietly: "Stay true to yourself."

They embraced. Without blame. Without promises. Simply – in silent understanding.

Sakura stood alone at the fork in the road.

The first step was a weight in her chest.
The second – silence.
The third – an unexpected lightness.
As if, right here, in solitude, she could hear her own voice again.

She looked back – no one was there. But warmth lingered in her heart.

"Some people are given to us to walk a part of the journey. And to leave light within us," she thought.
And she walked on.

Sometimes, loved ones leave not because they have stopped loving, but because their path calls them in another direction.
To let go is not to forget. It is to respect – their journey… and your own.

Yours, Sakura

Chapter 7. The City of Handcrafted Bridges

Sakura found herself in a city where each person built their own bridge.
Some wove theirs from delicate silk threads.
Others tied sturdy ropes.
Some chose steel cables.
Some – transparent threads of hope. Others – heavy iron chains.

And a few – golden strands, shimmering in the sunlight.
Everyone had their own.

It was along these bridges that people walked toward their dreams, toward love, success, or self-understanding.

But the rules here were strict:
"The stronger your bridge – the more you are worthy."
And also: "Do not stumble. Do not stop. Do not look down."

Sakura wove her bridge from the best threads – responsibility, diligence, logic, strength...
Every morning – a step. Every evening – a checkmark.
Her bridge was straight and precise. Too precise. As if she feared making even a single wrong knot.
And the farther she walked, the less she breathed. But she thought: this is how it must be. This is right. This is how everyone does it.

She did not walk – she fought.
Against fear. Against exhaustion. Against

herself.
Her hands were scraped, her eyes burned, her heart caged.
But from the outside, everything seemed perfect: step – checkmark, step – checkmark.

One day, the bridge began to tremble.
Perhaps from the wind. Perhaps from exhaustion.
Or perhaps because her heart could no longer remain silent.

But still, she walked. She clenched her teeth. She held on.
Until suddenly, there was a faint, almost imperceptible sound –
like a string snapping at the very core of her soul.

The bridge broke. Not with a crash. Not with drama.
Just – one moment she was sitting on a fragment.
Alone.
With empty hands.
A bare soul.
And the feeling that everything was lost.

But no one came to condemn her.
No one shouted: "You failed!"
There was no shame. No blame.
Only the wind. And the sky.

Sakura lifted her head.
And for the first time in a long while, she looked at the sky.
She had forgotten, in all the chaos of building a life,
how important it was – just to stop and look up.
Because it is in such simple, quiet moments
that true life is found.

And for the first time in a long while, Sakura cried.
Not because she was weak.
But because she was tired of being strong out of fear.
Fear of disappointment. Fear of falling short.
Fear of being insufficient.

Her tears did not destroy her.
They became a new thread.
True. Alive. Warm.

Sakura did not build a new bridge that day.
She simply lay on the ground.
And allowed herself to do nothing.
Not to rush.
Not to prove.
Not to fear.

She breathed. Simply breathed.
And for the first time in a long while – she felt alive.

We live in a world that teaches: "Move. Cope. Control."
But it does not teach us to stop when it hurts and simply let ourselves rest from the endless race.

Sometimes the only path to yourself is not a bridge.
It is a pause.
An exhale.
An exhale.
And silence.

Yours, Sakura

Chapter 8. The Window That No Longer Had Eyes

Sakura returned to the city of her childhood.
The old five-story building still stood. The same bench, the same path, the same windows.

And among all the windows, there was one she never forgot.
A window on the first floor.
An old woman always sat there.

As children, they feared her.
The children whispered:
– Witch. Strange. Silent. She just stares and stares…
They teased her.
Sometimes, they tossed twigs onto her windowsill and ran away.

Sakura was among them too.
Not the cruelest. Not the loudest.
But neither was she the one who stopped it.

She was simply afraid.
And then – she got used to it.
And then – she forgot.

Only when the old woman one day stopped appearing at the window,
something inside Sakura tightened.
Without explanation.
Without words.

Years passed.

And now, grown up, Sakura stood before that very window.
It was empty. Silent.
In the glass, her own reflection stared back – no longer a child. Now someone who understood.

– "She wasn't frightening," Sakura whispered.
– "She was lonely.
– She wasn't watching us – she was looking out at the world because there was nowhere else she could look.
– She didn't speak – because she couldn't.
– And we… we just didn't know. We didn't want to know."

Something trembled within her.

It wasn't guilt.
It was realization.

And perhaps, forgiveness – for the little girl she had been, who simply didn't know any better.

Sakura placed her hand against the glass and closed her eyes.

And suddenly, it felt as though, from the depths of time,
a gentle, almost inaudible voice whispered:
"You understood, after all. Thank you."

And if you understand – even years later –
that is already light.
And perhaps the one who silently waited always knew: one day, you will see.

Yours, Sakura

Chapter 9. The One They Forgot

Once, the lamp stood at the very heart of the home.
Its light gathered people, warmed the evenings, softened the silence.
It burned because it was needed. Because its flame was seen – and so was it.

But new times came.
The light became brighter. Faster. More convenient.
They said of it:
– "It's not the same anymore. Old."
And they moved it to a corner. And then – to the attic.
Without words. Without farewell.

There, beneath a layer of dust, it stood for years.
No one asked how it was.
And inside…
The wick dried…
The kerosene evaporated…
But something – warm, stubborn – would not let it go out.

That night, the city drowned in darkness.
Sakura stood by the window – in complete blackness.
All the familiar lights had gone out.
Phones didn't work, lamps were dead, screens were blank.
Inside her, it was dark too – as if this night mirrored something she had long hidden:
"I am no longer important. My voice is not needed. Am I… over?"

She didn't know why she went to the attic.
Her feet simply led her there.
To a place she hadn't been in ages.

There, beneath a blanket, she found the lamp.
She had forgotten it even existed.
Just as she had forgotten herself – the one who once dreamed. Who shone. Who burned.

Her hands trembled as she wiped away the dust.
The wick was slightly damp. Almost dry.
But still, she struck a match.

And in that moment –
the lamp lit up.

Hesitantly.
But – truly.

The light was faint.
But alive.
Like herself.

Sakura gazed at it – and tears filled her eyes.

– "I'm sorry I forgot you…" she whispered.
To the lamp.
And to herself.

Sometimes we are forgotten. And we begin to forget ourselves.
But even if your light has been hidden for a long time – it does not mean it is gone.
It waits.
Silently.
Deep within.
And one day, when true darkness falls – you remember
that you can still shine.

Yours, Sakura

Chapter 10. The One Who Waited for Her Father

As a child, Sakura disliked evenings.
When the sun set, fathers returned to the courtyard.
They lifted their children in their arms, spun them around,
hoisted them onto their shoulders.

And the children laughed.
They felt wanted. Expected. Loved.

Sakura stood in the courtyard too. Quietly.
With something in her hands that didn't matter.
She stroked a cat, traced shapes in the dirt with a stick,
looked away –
but always kept one eye on the entrance.
What if he came after all?...

But no one came.
And with each evening, something within her withered.
Not loudly.
But as though a part of her heart was learning to

be quiet.
Not to disturb. Not to ask.

Years passed.
Sakura grew up.
Strong. Convenient.
For everyone – except herself.

And then one day she found herself in that courtyard again,
where everything was hauntingly familiar:
the same bench, the same crack in the asphalt,
the same air – only no children's voices.

And suddenly, she saw her.
The girl.
Herself.

The child crouched,
drawing lines in the dirt with a stick,
still watching with one corner of her eye.
Still waiting.

Sakura's chest tightened.
She was afraid to approach.
The pain was too alive.

But she walked.
Slowly.
She sat down beside her.

– "You… are me?"
– "I have waited for you for so long.
I am not angry.
I was just lonely."

Sakura wept.
And whispered:
– "I'm sorry. I will never leave you again."

And suddenly she understood:
The girl had not been waiting for her father.
She had been waiting – for her.

Within each of us lives the one who once fell silent from pain.
If you dare to approach…
if you are not afraid…
and if you embrace her –
you will become yourself again.

Yours, Sakura

Chapter 11. Rainbow Leggings

At that time, Sakura still believed that being beautiful meant being like everyone else.
Wearing what others wore. Being noticed just as they were noticed.
The world seemed simple then: if you looked right, you would be loved.

Bright, rainbow-colored leggings were the dream of every girl in the courtyard.
They shimmered like candy wrappers, as if saying, "Look at me!"
When Sakura's mother bought her a pair, the girl was overjoyed.
It was a ticket to a special club – now she was "in style," now she was just like everyone else.

That same day, a few other girls wore their new leggings.
They all rushed to the boy they considered the most popular in the yard.

– "Choose who is the prettiest," they demanded. "But only one."

They straightened up, posed, put on their most charming smiles.
Sakura did her best too – this was her moment.

The boy walked slowly, like a great judge.
He looked at each girl, paused, compared.
And he did not choose Sakura.

She smiled, pretending nothing had happened.
But inside, something shattered.
As if a fragile part of her splintered into invisible shards.
And in her little pocket, a heavy stone settled –
a stone she would carry with her for many years.

From that day on, the leggings stopped being magical.
They no longer seemed special.
Sakura still wore them,
but now they were just clothes – fabric, colors, seams.
They no longer made her feel beautiful.

It took a long time to understand:
nothing on the outside can give you a sense of your own worth,
if you do not feel it within yourself.

But perhaps, it all began with those leggings.
With that childhood moment of "not you."
With that barely visible crack.
With that first turn
on the long path – to herself.

Sometimes within us
lives the one
who was once not chosen.
If you look her in the eyes…
smile…
and accept her –
she will bloom.

Yours, Sakura

Chapter 12. The Jacket the Color of Childhood

Sakura had a friend – not just any friend.
The kind you shared everything with: candies, secrets, even the same little pot.
They lived in the same courtyard, and each evening, they couldn't say goodbye –
walking each other back and forth, from the first building to the fifth and back again.
Laughter, whispers, steps on the asphalt... a friendship that seemed endless.

One day, the friend's mother bought her a new jacket.
Bright. Fancy. Almost magical.
Her friend shone in it like a little sun –
walked with her back straight, showed it off, and was afraid to stain it.

And at some point, something pricked at Sakura.
Something dark, aching, strange.
"Why does she have it, and I don't? And why does she keep showing it off?" Sakura thought.
She didn't say it aloud. But she thought it – and

that was enough.
Childish resentment, envy, frustration – all of it clenched in her chest and...
She pushed her friend.
Right into a muddy puddle.

The jacket was stained. Her friend burst into tears.
Afraid of her mother's anger. Hurt. Ran away...

And Sakura stood there, feeling not triumph. Not victory. But shame.
Burning, sticky, the kind you remember years later.
The kind that hides in the corners of your heart – not as punishment, but as a reminder:
where your weakness lies, and where your strength.

Years passed.
They were still friends.
They laughed, reminisced, embraced.
And only once, in passing, Sakura asked:
– "Do you remember that jacket?"
Her friend nodded and said:

– "Of course. But I forgave you long ago. I was bragging, wasn't I?"

They looked at each other – and they knew: this friendship had endured everything. Envy, quarrels, awkwardness, pain.
But it remained. Cleansed. Grown.

Sometimes true friendship is not just laughter.
It is also shame, confession, and the strength to say:
"I was wrong. But I am still here."

Yours, Sakura

Chapter 13. The Cake

When Sakura was little,
Aunt Olya lived next door.
Kind, smiling, with the scent of vanilla.

Every year on Sakura's birthday,
she would bring her
a big, homemade Napoleon cake.

Soft, layered,
with cream that melted in the mouth.
It smelled of milk, warmth, and celebration.
The cake was always whole –
and just for her.

Sakura looked forward to it more than any gift,
waiting for that special moment:
the crinkling box,
Aunt Olya's voice:
– "Happy birthday, sunshine."

She believed
that the celebration truly began
with that little slice of happiness.

Time passed.
Sakura grew older,
and Aunt Olya grew quieter.

First, she stopped bringing the cake.
Then she visited less often.
And one day,
her door remained closed forever.

Only the scent of vanilla
would sometimes linger in the air –
like a memory
that hadn't yet let go.

Sakura stopped waiting
for birthdays with the same excitement.
Something in those days
became quieter.

Years went by.
And one day,
on Sakura's birthday as an adult,
a dear friend baked her a cake.

Homemade. Napoleon.
A gift – from the heart.

And when Sakura
took the first bite,
something within her opened.
Tenderness appeared.
A piercing gratitude.

This is what I was missing…

Sometimes we lose something important –
and we don't even notice.
The taste of celebration.
The scent of love.
Someone's gesture
that made a day special.

But one day,
someone, without even knowing,
gives it back to you.
And you suddenly remember
what it feels like:
to know you are loved.
For no reason.
Truly.

Yours, Sakura

Chapter 14. Where the Stage Begins with the Heart

Sometimes, fate does not simply send friends your way –
it brings you battle sisters.
The kind with whom you can laugh until your stomach aches,
and keep walking, even when the whole world says, "You can't."

Sakura was sixteen,
and that was when she met her –
a girl with fire in her eyes and a stubborn heart.
They studied to become veterinarians –
crammed microbiology and Latin, fed dogs at the shelter,
sipped tea from plastic cups, and dreamed.

Dreamed loudly. Like music.

One evening –
a free concert, the city's noise, a crowd.
And on stage – the artist whose music lived in their headphones.
Their hearts beat louder than the bass.

Her friend whispered:
– "Want to get closer?"
– "Of course."

And so, they – two girls,
simply walked up to the police officers and asked:
– "Could we… go there, past the barrier?"
No arrogance. No fear. Just honesty.
And… they heard in reply:
– "Go ahead."

They walked through.
The crowd remained behind.
They passed the guards, passed the metal detectors,
climbed the stairs leading backstage –
as if the whole world had decided: "Let them in."
No one stopped them.

It was as if the inner stage –
the one that begins not with a spotlight,
but with an open heart –
suddenly aligned with the real one.

The artist turned around:
– "Uh… who are you? How did you get here?"

– "Us? We're just two girls who love your
music. Just for a moment. Just an autograph."

He laughed.
– "Alright. Just not on stage."

But… they had no paper.
Everything had happened so spontaneously.
Only their microbiology textbook –
thick, worn, smelling of ink and sleepless nights.

And so – on a blank page,
a sweeping line appeared:
"Hello to the librarian of the College of
Veterinary Medicine."
And his autograph.

Then came the usual end of the school year…
which meant…
They returned the textbook to the library.
It became part of someone else's studies.
But somewhere between bacteria and viruses –
lived the story of how true courage is simply
going and asking.
How the stage begins not with a ticket,
but with an open gaze.

How even the most ordinary day
can leave a starry trace.

The world responds to those
who walk with trust,
not with a plan to break through walls.
And suddenly, you find:
you are already where you dreamed of being.

Yours, Sakura

Chapter 15. The Pink Cat
Once, when Sakura was very little,
she had a dream.
In that dream, a pink cat came to her.
It was fluffy, warm,
and looked at her with such love,
as if it had known her all its life.

Sakura woke up and immediately ran to her mother:
– "Mama, mama, I saw a pink cat in my dream!

It was real!
I really want it to be mine!"

All day, she spoke only of this.
About its soft paws,
about how it looked at her,
about how much she was waiting for it.
And even when her mother gently said:
– "Sweetheart, such cats probably don't exist…"
Sakura shook her head:
– "No, mama. It does. I believe."

That day, while playing at home,
she still thought about it.
And then it was time to go for a walk.
Sakura opened the front door –
and froze.

On the doormat, right at the doorstep,
sat a cat.

Not bright pink, not cartoonish,
but creamy, like the color of an evening cloud,
the closest possible shade of pink that nature
could create.
It looked at her as if it had known her all its life.
Just like in her dream.

No one knew where it came from.
But it came – just for her.

From that moment, they were inseparable.
The cat was extraordinarily affectionate.
It allowed itself to be swaddled,
placed in a stroller, carried on her back,
and even seemed to fall asleep –
like a child.

They loved each other –
quietly, in a special way.
The way only children and animals can.

And Sakura remembered this for her whole life:
if you believe truly,
with love, with a pure heart –
even a pink cat can appear in this world.

Yours, Sakura

Chapter 16. The Story That Never Existed

When Sakura was in elementary school,
one summer gifted her a quiet wonder.
She met a boy,
and their friendship was simple and beautiful –
like the evening breeze in a field.

They laughed,
shared candies,
and at the school dance, he chose to dance with her –
to the slowest, most tender songs.

In that moment, Sakura thought:
everything she needed was already there.
Light, attention, the feeling
that she was special.

And then autumn came.
And a new boy was transferred to her class.
It was him.

They recognized each other instantly.
But instead of joy –
a quiet tension.

They seemed to fall silent at the same time.
They looked at each other
and didn't know how to return
to that simple, summer feeling.

Over time, they began talking again.
There was a shared group of friends,
conversations, games.
But inside, Sakura always thought:
"What if he doesn't like me anymore?"
The story seemed to crumble,
never truly beginning.

Years passed.
Sakura left, grew up, lived.
And one day, returning to her hometown,
she accidentally met him.
The same boy.
Now – a grown man.

They walked through the evening city,
talked about school, life,
about how everything had changed.

And suddenly he said:
– "You know…
back then, I had nothing to offer you.

You were so… so bright, so real.
And I… I felt
like I didn't belong by your side.
I thought I wasn't enough for you.
So I stayed silent."

Sakura looked at the sky for a long time.
There were no stars –
but a quiet calm surrounded them.

Sometimes stories do not happen
not because you weren't enough.
But because the other person
did not feel enough beside you.

There are moments
when you think:
"I must have not been enough…"

But in truth –
you were simply too real
for those who were not yet ready.

You were never "too much."
You were – yourself.
And that is always
more than enough.

Yours, Sakura

Chapter 17. Health to Your Hands

Sakura met her in a foreign country,
where everything felt new and unfamiliar.
It was the beginning of a long journey of adaptation –
with a strange language, new rules,
and a longing for home.
And it was then that fate brought this friend into her life.

She had hands in which the sun seemed to live.

Her friend never asked unnecessary questions.
She just showed up whenever she sensed
that someone nearby was struggling.
She would come when the children fell ill,
bring medicine,
cook fragrant homemade food.
She did it all so effortlessly,
as if helping was not a task, but a breath.
As if kindness
was her very nature.

She never did it for show.
Her actions carried no grand words –

just a quiet care that could be felt.
A simple, genuine soul.

And at her house, there was always hot tea –
fragrant, spicy, warm.
And little bowls with nuts, dried fruit,
small treats
in which the very joy of meeting seemed to dwell.
Sitting at her table meant feeling, once again,
that you were not just a passing guest in this home.
You were accepted without conditions.

Sakura often wondered:
Where did she get all that light?
Her generosity didn't come from abundance,
but from the heart.
She shared what she had,
without waiting for anyone to ask.
And that made life a little easier –
to live, to believe, to hope.

Whenever Sakura tried to thank her,
she remembered her grandmother's words:
"May your hands never ache."

But her friend, who came from a sunlit country, would smile softly and say:

– "We say it differently.
Health to your hands."

Since then, Sakura would repeat those words whenever kindness appeared.
Like a prayer.
Like gratitude.
Like acknowledgment.

May there be more hands like these.
May such friends meet each of us –
and stay.
Like light.
Like a miracle.

Yours, Sakura

Chapter 18. A Samurai Has No Goal, Only a Path

Sometimes life brings you a person –
one who makes you feel
the sound of the world.

In Sakura's life, there was such a person.
Now his soul is somewhere high above,
where stars shine and silence sings.
But he remains within her –
in every breath, every look at the sky,
every frame where light lives.

He owned restaurants – not for fame.
Brewed rare beer – not for profit.
He filled everything around him with meaning.
As if every act was an extension of his soul.

But most of all, he spoke through music.
A saxophone in his hands didn't shout – it sang
from the soul.
Sometimes with warm breath, sometimes with longing,
sometimes like the whisper of an autumn breeze.
He played in a way that made the music seep

under your skin.
It touched something deep inside you, something you didn't know was there.
He didn't play for the stage. He just played.
And that was – real.

But the most important thing was the space he created with his presence.
You could be silent with him –
and it felt like another world opened up.
Quiet. Deep. Infinite.
He was a friend. A mentor.
An entire ocean.

He knew:
Taste is an art.
Sound is a prayer.
Life is not a stage. Life is a path.

And sometimes that path is not straight.
You get tired. You doubt.
And suddenly, beside you – a person
who doesn't push, doesn't advise –
just offers a shoulder.
Silently. Calmly.
Only those whose soul is like a universe do that.

When Sakura began taking photographs,
she dreamed of a rare lens.
One day, she casually mentioned it to him.

Some time passed.
A phone call:
– "Come downstairs. The driver has something for you."

A box. Inside – that very lens.
Rare. Almost unattainable.
No words. No explanations.
Not just a thing – a gesture.
Quiet, like music. Strong, like a lesson.

From that day, her photos changed.
They had more soul. More light. More life.

A samurai has no goal, only a path.
And sometimes – his step becomes someone else's beginning.

Yours, Sakura

Chapter 19. The One Who Showed Not a Map, but the Road

Sometimes a Teacher doesn't just come to class.
He walks into your life –
with the scent of moss, mountain wind,
and eyes that reflect the Carpathians.

That's how it was when Sakura was in fifth grade.
He arrived – the new geography teacher.
No boring diagrams, no dry formulas.
With a hiking backpack and a stack of photographs.
He spoke of Petros
and the old observatory in the mountains –
a place where people once gazed at the stars,
and where, even now,
the very air seems to hold a dream
of something vast and infinite.

Geography stopped being just a subject.
It became the sound of a stream,
the rustle of a map on a desk,
the feeling that you were part of something big.

He didn't force us to learn –
he made us fall in love.
We studied not for grades,
but because living and discovering the world
was simply exciting.

And then there were the mountains.
A club, tents, raincoats.
Sakura spent her first night in a tent.
She listened as, at night,
sheep wandered across the slopes,
and stared into the fire –
where the dreams of those who followed it
were ignited.

He wasn't just a teacher.
He was a guide to real life.
A person you wanted to follow –
not out of fear,
but because being near him made you feel:
you had strength within you.

Then he was gone.
And it became as quiet
as it is after a song
you didn't want to end.

But he remained.
In everyone who had sat at his desk.
In those who, one day, dared –
and followed their dreams.
He stayed where
he once lit a light.

Sometimes a person comes into the world
not just to live their own life,
but to ignite dozens of others.

Yours, Sakura

Chapter 20. As Long as Her Voice Sings

Some evenings do not shine with lamps.
Yet they are the warmest.
Some memories do not dazzle with brightness.
Yet they light our lives forever.

In Sakura's house, the electricity would go out
almost every evening –

a common occurrence in their country.
Sometimes she managed to finish her homework.
Sometimes – she wrote by candlelight.
And sometimes – she simply sat in the darkness.

But it was then that the most magical time would begin.

Her grandmother.
With piercing blue eyes, in which you could drown – or find the sky.
With warm, gentle hands that smelled of mint and old paper.
With a voice like a lullaby sung by the soul itself.

They would sit together.
Sometimes by the faint glow of a kerosene lamp.
Sometimes – by a candle.
And sometimes – simply in the dark.

And her grandmother would sing.
Romances – those old songs where someone's fate lived in every note.
Stories of love. Of parting. Of hope.
Songs that didn't shout – they whispered straight to the heart.

Sakura sat quietly.
Afraid to breathe too loudly, so as not to disturb the magic.
The darkness outside seemed soft.
The room – alive.
And the whole world seemed to pause, just to listen.

She didn't understand all the words, but she felt everything.
With every cell of her being.
With every shadow within her.
Because her grandmother wasn't just singing – she was healing the silence.

Her grandmother is gone now.
But her voice… Sakura still hears it.
It lives in her memory.
It sings when the world is dark.
When there is pain. When she needs warmth.
All she has to do is close her eyes –
and her grandmother is there again.
Like a light
that cannot be turned off.

Sometimes light doesn't go out outside, but within.
But if you remember those who loved you –
the darkness retreats.

Yours, Sakura

Chapter 21. The One Who Lives Under the Couch

When Sakura was a student,
she lived with a friend in a small, rented apartment.
During the day, they laughed, dreamed, and pretended
they were already adults.

But in the evening, when it was time to turn off the light,
they suddenly remembered
that little girls still lived within them.

Because the moment they pressed the switch –
their hearts would start beating faster.

They had to leap –
in one quick jump onto the bed,
before he came out.

The one who lived under the couch.

They even gave him a name.
He was almost friendly,
almost imaginary.
Sometimes they even laughed at him,
teased each other –
yet still jumped,
lifting their feet off the ground,
as if he really existed.

It was only much later that Sakura realized –
the one who lived under the couch –
he never truly left.
He moved with them to new apartments,
hiding not just in the dark,
but in memory.
He became less visible,
but still grabbed at their ankles
whenever they feared taking a step into the unknown,
whenever they doubted themselves,

whenever they listened to someone else's voice
more than their own.

He lives in each of us,
until we turn on the light – not in the room –
but within ourselves.

And now, as an adult,
Sakura sometimes sees
how her own children
pull their feet up onto the bed
or tiptoe to the switch,
as if something hides in the darkness.

And Sakura smiles.
Apparently, they know about him too.
About the one who lives under the couch.
About the creature whose name is almost never spoken,
like Voldemort in an old tale.

Perhaps he is just a reminder:
that all of us – even adults –
were once children.
And so, in each of us,
there is a little corner
where the one who lives under the couch still dwells.

Yours, Sakura

Chapter 22. Once – and Never Again

When Sakura became a mother,
she often remembered a conversation with her aunt.
Her aunt had told her a story
that settled quietly, without reproach,
in Sakura's heart forever.

In her youth, her aunt had a beautiful little girl.
Beloved, long-awaited, a child made of light.
But soon her husband had to leave for work abroad,
and she, following him, couldn't take the child along.
The baby stayed with the grandmother – just for a while.
For a few months.

But time suddenly stretched.
And it was enough
for her to later say with sadness:
– "I didn't see her take her first steps,
discover the world,

laugh, or learn to speak.
And it will never happen again."

Sakura listened and remembered.
And when she had her own children,
those words suddenly resurfaced,
like a letter from the past.
She caught every funny conclusion they made,
every phrase they spoke with a mistake,
every attempt to understand this strange adult world.
Because she knew:
today is not a rehearsal.
Today is the only time.

Children grow not by days –
but by glances.
By "Mom, look!"
By the first "I can do it myself."
And one day, morning comes,
when you let them go into their own lives.

You know they will fly.
You don't hold them back.
But you remember every spring,
when they were still in the nest.

And Sakura often whispered to herself:
catch this moment.
Look into their eyes.
Remember the scent of their hair.
Once – and never again.

Because children don't remember how many toys they had.
They remember how much you were there.
And the most important things in life don't happen loudly.
They pass by, if you don't watch.
And only later, they become priceless.

Yours, Sakura

Chapter 23. The Bird

When Sakura was about six,
she spent her summer in a seaside town.
In warm courtyards, under the murmur of waves,
she discovered something new every day.

One day, she saw a bird.
It sat in the shade of an old tree –
alone, ruffled,
and one of its wings hung awkwardly low.

– "Let's help it," –
Sakura pleaded with her grandmother.

They brought the bird home.
Fed it, nursed it, spoke to it in whispers.
The wing healed slowly.
With each day, life returned to it.

And then one day, her grandmother said:
– "The time has come.
A bird is a creature of freedom.
It cannot live in a cage,
even if the cage is kind."

Sakura opened the window.
The bird hesitated for a moment,
then flapped its strong wing –
and flew away.

The girl's heart tightened.
The emptiness beyond the window felt vast.

But the next day,
a flock of birds appeared at the windowsill.
Sakura immediately recognized her –
the one she had saved.

She stayed closer than the others.
Looked attentively, ate from her hand,
and seemed to say:
"I remember."

At that moment, Sakura suddenly understood:
love is not about holding on.
Love is trust.
When you let go with kindness –
there is space for return.

Sometimes we are so afraid to lose,
that we hold too tightly.

But true closeness
is born not in fear,
but in freedom.

If you let go with love –
those who are truly yours
will always return.
Of their own will.
With gratitude.
With trust.

Yours, Sakura

Chapter 24. Ashen Light

It was a time
when diaries smelled of ink,
and love lived in school corridors –
in accidental glances,
in unexplored feelings.

In the evenings, Sakura would light candles.
Not for light –
but for silence.
Candles knew how to stay close
when memories unfolded,
like a melody without words.

There was someone in her life.
Not the one meant by fate.
But the one meant by inspiration.

He probably never knew
how her heart sounded at that moment –
when they listened to the same notes.

She wrote.
Poems. Thoughts.

Music in words.
And she resonated.

Their friendship grew quietly, between the lines.
It no longer exists now –
years, distances.
But that short story
was enough to stay with her forever.
Sometimes a single note
is enough for the music to live in you all your life.

One evening,
looking at the Moon –
thin, almost disappearing –
Sakura saw it begin to glow.
Softly. Almost imperceptibly.

Ashen light.

Some say it's just the Earth's reflected glow.
But an old legend knows something else…

"It is feelings
that did not demand a response.
It is gratitude
that became light.

It is love
that took nothing –
but left wings behind."

Sakura smiled.
Not because she was waiting.
But because she knew:
some encounters are meant
to give you so much light
that it's enough to share with others.

Yours, Sakura

Chapter 25. Where the Wind Begins

Sometimes what we lack is not strength – but air.
Not plans – but space.
Not support – but the right to simply breathe fully.

On her birthday, Sakura's friend gave her something unexpected:

— "It's a horseback riding lesson," she said. "I know you'll love it."

Sakura approached – and felt the quiet presence of a living force beside her,
ready to burst into a gallop at the slightest hint.
The horse stood calmly, but in that calm was power.
And in her mind, a familiar voice whispered:
"You're an adult now. You have other responsibilities. Why do you need this foolishness?"
"You are not that little girl anymore. You've learned to live quietly, properly, sensibly…"

But her hand reached out on its own.
And when she touched the warm neck – her heart took a breath.
Deep. Real.
As if a voice from the depths of her soul whispered:
"You are free. You always were.
Just remember."

She climbed into the saddle. Her heart raced, her breath unsteady.

The horse took a step… another…
And suddenly – a leap. Gallop.

Her body leaned forward, the wind struck her face.
Her hair flew back –
and with it, everything else fell away:
tension, fear, doubt.
Laughter burst out on its own – sincere, ringing.
Tears stung her eyes. Not from pain. From relief.
From finally allowing herself to be alive.
She wasn't riding – she was flying.
And in that flight was everything:
joy, strength, and a childlike, almost forgotten belief
that the world could still be kind.

That day, Sakura understood:
Freedom is not a place. It is a state of being.
It is within.
But you can only reach it if you let go of fear.
And allow yourself to trust the wind.

Sometimes the miracle is not wings.
Sometimes the miracle is someone handing you the reins
and saying:
"Trust. The wind is already waiting."

Yours, Sakura

Chapter 26. The Queen's Gambit

Sakura was sitting in a warm Italian café,
where sunlight spilled down the walls,
and the scent of basil mingled with the evening air.

Beside her was a woman –
vibrant, like a brushstroke on canvas,
confident, like a final chord.
With red lipstick and sparks in her eyes,
she seemed to blend together
a love for life, a passion for books,
and a deep longing for art.
Being near her felt like an invitation –
to stop pretending, to stop hesitating,
and simply be yourself.

Sakura remembered how they raced along the Venetian canals
in a private water taxi,
sang an old Italian love song,
and called out to passing boats:
"Ti amo!"

And people smiled in return,
as if that joy was impossible not to share.

Later, in that same café,
the woman suddenly fell silent
and spoke in a different tone –
quiet, almost personal.
The kind of tone you share with those who will understand.

– "Sometimes it's hard for me," she said.
– "And when it truly becomes difficult,
I imagine a woman
who feels perfectly at home in this moment.
Confident. Whole.
As if she was born for this situation."

– "And I ask myself:
'What would she do?'
And I wear her like a mood.
Like a posture.
Like a gaze.
And I act.
Because if she could –
then so can I."

Sakura stayed silent.
But inside, something trembled.
Because she too was afraid.
She too wanted to be someone
whose eyes held light, not shadows.

Since then, whenever things got hard,
Sakura remembered that meeting.
And in her mind, the familiar question appeared:
"What would the woman who feels confident and free do?"
And then – softer, deeper:
"What would I do – if I believed in myself?"

And each time,
answering that question,
Sakura took a step.
A small one.
Bold and her own.

Yours, Sakura

Chapter 27. Paper Birds

When Sakura was little and waiting for her to arrive,
she never mistook that ring for any other.
She knew, it was her.
She would leap up, rush to the door, and shout:

– "My Cat Aunt is here!"

And she would throw herself into her arms – with all her heart.

She only ever called her that.
Because her aunt was like a cat:
smart, direct, with a strong character.
She spoke honestly – where others would stay silent.
And if she loved – she loved forever.

When Sakura visited her,
the courtyard seemed to breathe with her warmth:
the old bench, the playground, the little shop by the entrance.
Every detail – a part of her.

One day, her aunt said:

– "They've delivered fresh bread. Will you run and get some?"

Sakura ran, broke off the warm crust.
And when her aunt saw the crumpled paper bag, she smiled:

– "Couldn't resist? And you're right.
Warm bread is meant to be torn right away."

And then – the orphanage.
Her Cat Aunt became a mother to those who had none.
Children came to her – with pain, with truth.
And if any adult caused them harm –
she stood between them.
Firmly. Until the end.

When her Cat Aunt passed away,
her husband was the first to enter the room.
He saw…
And he cried out.
Called her name. Wept.
As if half his heart had been torn out.

As if love hadn't finished speaking.
As if she could still be brought back.

A month later, he was gone too.
No words. No illness.
Just – followed her.

Women like her are loved not until the end of life –
but until the end of love.
And if it is real,
it never ends.

Sakura ran her hand along the old bench.
Once, they had sat here together,
talking about life.

And then her aunt had said:

– "People are like paper birds.
Fragile. Delicate.
And yet – capable of flight.
You will never know if you can fly
until you spread your wings."

And Sakura understood:
her wings – were from her.
From her Cat Aunt.

When someone like those leaves –
an emptiness remains.
But time passes,
and suddenly you hear her voice –
in your own.
Feel her strength –
in how you hold another's hand.
And you realize:
you didn't just remember.
You continue.

Yours, Sakura

Chapter 28. All Roads – A Web Leading to Yourself

Sometimes Sakura sat by the window with a cup of tea.
Watched the raindrops run down the glass.
And suddenly... she remembered.

Memory came quietly,
without an invitation.
It sat beside her.
And pulled out what she had hidden.

If she had submitted her documents to where her heart truly led,
not where it was "right" or easier.
If she hadn't been afraid of difficulty.
If she had chosen herself –
not what was convenient for others.

If she hadn't crossed out her dream,
just because no one believed in it.
Not even she did.

If she hadn't stayed,
hadn't pretended everything was fine,
but simply said:
"It's unbearably quiet inside me here."

If she hadn't left that job,
where it was hard –
but her heart lived.

If she had said:
"I love you,"

while there was still someone to hear it.
Or stayed that moment,
when someone was waiting,
and she turned away –
out of fear, pride, or pain.

If she had followed herself –
not the expectations of others.
If she had left sooner.
Or stayed – just a little longer.

Everyone has their "what if."
Sakura had many.
Some had names.
Others – voices.
Some smelled of a foreign city,
and some – of a home she never chose.

She sat –
and felt a life being born inside her that she hadn't lived.
But remembered.
Right down to the laughter she never heard.
To the hands she never held.

Strange – she hadn't lived that life,
yet it lived within her.

And then it seemed: everything inside was a web.
Thin. Alive.
Every thread – a crossroad.

Sakura understood:
a person is not just their steps.
A person is also what they ran from.
What they didn't dare.
What they let go.

She was the girl by the stage.
And the woman who didn't board the train.
And the one who got everything wrong –
and never said the most important thing.

These weren't mistakes. They were a map.
Complex. Alive. Her own.

We don't always choose correctly.
But if we walk honestly –
everything leads to ourselves.
To the one who can keep walking, even when afraid.
Who doesn't hide from shadows.
And breathes – however they can.
Without loud words. But truly.

Yours, Sakura

Chapter 29. Where Every Step Echoes

You cannot see them with your eyes,
but they hang over everyone.
Every "it's nothing" that caused pain
stays in the air. And waits.

In this world, above people –
a sky full of marks.

Invisible to the eye,
they hover above,
like silent signs –
bright, faded, heavy.

Each mark is no accident.
It is a trace.
Left where a person caused pain.

One for a look that carried mockery,
settling in someone's heart like dust that cannot
be wiped away.
Another for an animal
left on the roadside, while the driver never
looked back.
A third for a child's cry,

silenced by harsh words spoken "in a bad mood"
—

and since then, the child grew quieter.
Not because they matured.
But because life became frightening.

For those whose hearts
once tightened – because of us.
For those we didn't help,
though we could have.
For those we hurt with words,
and then forgot.
For those whose pain we dismissed.
Whose feelings we mocked.
Whose silence we ignored.

Each of these actions –
a drop of dark resin.
It does not disappear.
It clings.
And with each day –
it becomes heavier.

The more of these traces,
the denser the air.
As if it pulls a person down.

Their steps slow.
Their shoulders hunch.
Even laughter sounds muffled –
as if through water.

People do not understand
why each year it is harder to breathe,
to listen, to rise from bed.
They search for the reason in the body.
But the reason is – in the traces.

And then comes the day,
when this weight becomes unbearable.
The body forgets how to walk.
The gaze fades.
A person ceases to be themselves.
They no longer walk.
They crawl.
And then – simply lie.
Silent.
And never rise again.

Not from age.
But from the pain they left behind.
From the emptiness they created.

From the weight of themselves, which they
could no longer bear.

But I have seen others…

Those whose marks also existed.
But they were bright – like a breath after tears.
Clear – like morning after a long night.

They stumbled too.
But they rose –
and walked on,
only differently.
Softer. With more care.

Each of their actions –
a gentle hand on a wound.
Not loud.
But with hope.

The choice remains.
Not to seem good.
But to remain alive.
Human.
One whose step
doesn't leave cracks,
but leaves a path.
For others.

Yours, Sakura

Chapter 30. The Room Where Words Wait

In one house, there was a room where unspoken words were stored.
It was not visible.
But it existed for everyone.

Into it flew the phrases never spoken in time.
– "I miss you."
– "I'm scared."
– "I'm sorry."
– "Thank you for being there."
They settled on the floor, on shelves, on the ceiling.
Quietly. Silently. Yet heavily.

Sakura did not know about this room.
But one night she woke up, feeling a weight in her chest,
as if something inside her refused to let go.
She closed her eyes – and it was as if she fell into a space that was familiar... but forgotten.

Before her stood a door. Old. With a worn handle.
She reached for it –

and something in her chest trembled – like the scent of silence, where forgotten words are kept.

The room was filled with letters, scraps, whispers.
Words she had never said.

On the floor lay a note.
Yellowed, crumpled, with corners stuck together by tears.

"Mom, I was so scared when you shouted that time.
I wanted to tell you that I just felt bad.
But you left. And I went silent. Forever."

Nearby – a small paper bundle.

"I miss you, Dad. Even though I pretend I don't care."

On an old, folded page – written in childish handwriting, tilted letters:

"Let's go for a walk again… maybe I'll see him. Just to look at him from afar."

On the windowsill – a curled ribbon:

"I love you. I just… didn't know how to say it first."

Sakura's fingers brushed the ribbon – and her heart clenched.
She remembered:
The street by the school.
Old trees, their autumn yellow leaves rustling beneath her feet.
And him – that boy – standing by the school fence.
Looking at her. Waiting.
He said nothing – just waited.
Her heart pounded in her throat.

But she didn't approach.
She smiled – and walked away.
Because she didn't believe she could be loved.
Because she was afraid.

In the corner lay another note, folded in half, with neat, girlish handwriting:

"We're dating. I didn't know how to tell you. I hope you understand."

Sakura recognized the handwriting immediately.
It was her friend's.
The same one who had recently giggled:

"How can you like him? He's so ugly. Are you serious? Ugh."

Back then, Sakura swallowed her feelings, pretending nothing happened.
Acted like she didn't care.
But inside – something tightened forever.

And now – this note.
Like a knife pressed into the same old wound.

She didn't scream.
She simply felt trust breaking silently.
And how the bitterness of silence became a habit.

Sakura sat on the floor.
Surrounded by letters.
Some screamed. Others whispered.
But all of them held what she once chose not to say.

She brushed her hand across the floor.
And whispered:

– "I didn't know how to speak. I thought silence would protect me.
– But now I understand: all these words stayed inside me.
– And they still want to be spoken."

She stood up.
And spoke to herself:

I forgive.
Myself.
And those who stayed silent beside me.
And those who hurt with words.
And those who didn't hear.
I don't want to keep all this inside anymore.
I want to be alive and free.

There is a room of silence in everyone.
But one day you can open it.
And start taking the words out – one by one.
To live – not in silence.
But in truth.

Yours, Sakura

Chapter 31. The Station of Unsubmitted Trains

Somewhere between cities, there is a station
that appears on no map.
There – silence. Dust. And trains that never leave.
Not because they are late.
But because no one ever submitted tickets for them.

Sakura found herself there by chance.
Or – perhaps when it was no longer possible to stay silent.
She walked along the platform,
as if searching for something
she herself had forgotten.

Benches stood along the platform.
On one of them – a pile of folded tickets.
Each one – someone's unsaid words.

"Mom, I was scared when you shouted...
I just wanted you to hug me, not walk away."

"Dad, I miss you.
Even though I pretend I'm fine."

"I love you. I just… didn't know how to say it first."

The tickets lay quietly.
Like words that were never spoken in time.
That remained – inside.

Sakura picked one up.
It was crumpled, the corner marked with a trace of tears.
She recognized it at once: it was hers.
Her own.
Once unsaid – and left here.

In another corner of the hall was a bench,
and on it – a bundle of crumpled notes:

"We're dating. I didn't know how to tell you.
I hope you understand."

Sakura knew the handwriting.
It was her friend's.
The one who laughed when she found out who Sakura liked.
And she was the one who took him later.

Without explaining. Without asking.
Leaving only silence.

Sakura sat beside the bench.
Everything lying around her
was not just the past.
These were her unsubmitted tickets.
Words that could have taken her to another life.
But she hadn't boarded that train.

Beside her stood a quiet Attendant.
He didn't speak. Didn't rush her.
He simply was.
Like the silence in which you can finally hear
yourself.

Sakura took one of the tickets.
And whispered:

– "I didn't know how to speak.
I thought silence would protect me.
But now I know:
everything I didn't say
still stayed inside me.
And it wants to be heard."

She stood.
And approached the ticket counter.
She placed the old ticket on the counter.

– "I won't go where there is regret.
I will go where words begin to be spoken."

And in that moment, one of the trains
gave a soft, distant hum.
For the first time in a long while.

Each of us has our own station.
With compartments filled with unsaid words.
With trains we never boarded.

But one day you can return.
And speak.
Even one word.
And then – the train will move.

Yours, Sakura

Chapter 32. One Day, the House Fell Silent

It was the first winter of their life together when Sakura and her beloved brought home a small, white, fluffy miracle. She arrived in that same year when they first decided they wanted to be a family – to share not only the joys but also the burdens of each passing day. They carried her across the threshold, opened the door, and their world filled with the soft, gentle sound of tiny paws, the soothing hum of quiet purring, and the curious, watchful gaze of bright, knowing eyes.

From that moment on, she became not just a pet but a true member of their family, a companion on the endless road of life. She witnessed their home fill with laughter, their hearts overflow with love, and their dreams either blossom or shatter against the harsh stones of reality. She was always there, never asking for more than the warmth of their company, gracefully leaping from windowsill to soft couch, leaving behind a whisper of movement, like a trail of sunlit dust.

When Sakura first returned home with her newborn in her arms, the little cat, as if sensing the profound shift in the air, approached the crib. Without a sound, she leaped inside, curled up at the baby's feet, and began to purr softly, wrapping the fragile new life in a warm cocoon of her own heartbeat. From that day on, she became the child's silent guardian – warming him through cold nights, watching over his dreams, and perhaps even singing him gentle lullabies when no one else was looking.

And when Sakura herself fell ill, the cat would come to her side, softly pressing her warm body against her legs, or quietly settling beside her, never demanding, only offering her silent, comforting presence. She became her quiet strength, her faithful companion, her patient, watchful friend.

Years passed. Cities changed, countries came and went, homes transformed, and landscapes outside their windows blurred into each other. Yet, the cat remained, following them to each new address, reminding them that a true home is not just walls and a roof, but those who share the journey with you – those who stand by you through every joy and sorrow.

But one day, everything changed. The cat fell ill. At first, it was just small signs – a loss of appetite, a slowing step, a faint sigh in the night. But then the illness began to steal her strength swiftly, draining the light from her eyes, robbing her of the graceful movements that once defined her.

And then, one day, the house fell into a deep, suffocating silence. A silence that presses on the heart, that makes every echo of a footstep feel like a ghost from the past, that turns every corner into a painful reminder of what has been lost. Sakura found herself sitting on the cold floor of an empty room, feeling that silence seep into her skin, slowly draining the warmth she had once known.

They took her to the vet, who, with a resigned shrug, suggested they ease her suffering, to make that final choice. But Sakura and her beloved shook their heads.

"We are not ones to take the easy way out. She has been with us all her life, filling our home with warmth and light. And now, when she needs us the most, we cannot betray her by choosing a quick, easy path, simply because it is hard or painful to watch her suffer. We will stay by her side, just as she has always stayed by ours. We will hold her paw as long as she has the strength to take even one more small step. We will be grateful for every day when her eyes still find ours, for every gentle touch of her soft fur, for every quiet purr in the night."

And so, they chose to fight. For two more months, they surrounded her with love, carried her into the warm sunlight, so she could feel its gentle warmth on her snowy fur. They fed her the tastiest treats, stroked her soft coat, and whispered words of gratitude for every moment spent together.

And only when the final spark of life had left her eyes, when her breathing had become so faint it could barely be felt, did they finally understand that it was time to say goodbye. She slipped away quietly, surrounded by their love, her tiny heart coming to rest as the house fell silent once more.

But even after her departure, they continued to hear her soft steps on the old wooden floors, to glimpse her shadow in the curtain's folds, to feel her warmth in the patches of sunlight scattered across the living room floor. Her memory remained, present in every corner, in every whisper of the wind, in every breath of their home.

And then, one ordinary evening, as Sakura sat alone in the quiet of their living room, she felt something soft brush against her leg. For just a moment, it felt as though her loyal cat had returned to say one final "thank you."

And in that moment, Sakura understood:

Loss is not an emptiness, but a trace left behind by love.

It is the warmth that comforted us for years.

It is the gentle steps upon old wooden floors.

It is the soft purring in the quiet of the night.

It is the gratitude for every single day we shared.

Love is not just what we receive but also what we give.

Every moment spent together is a gift to be cherished.

We gave her warmth, and she filled our days with light.

We cared for her, and she taught us to be kind, patient, and devoted.

And though each of us must one day leave this world, the traces of our love remain forever – in every corner of our home, in every ray of sunlight, in every quiet breath of the night.

We will all leave someday, but while we are here, we have the chance to make this journey a little brighter for one another. And perhaps that is the greatest miracle of life.

Yours, Sakura

Chapter 33. The Mirror of the Edge: Before You Disappear

They say the Keeper of the Mirror of the Edge lives nowhere.
He appears in silence – wherever a person is about to disappear.
He doesn't save you.
He is simply there,
so that you – for the first time in a long while – remember yourself.

Sakura walked along a path among forest and stones.
No voices, no signs.
Only the wind, dry grasses,
and the earth breathing beneath her feet.

There are days
when even waking up is a triumph.
When the silence within you screams louder than any voice.
When you keep going but no longer know why.

She wasn't looking for a miracle.
She just wanted a silence
where she didn't have to be strong.

They said: if you reach the very edge –
one more step and you vanish,
you may meet him.

He doesn't speak.
He doesn't explain.
He is – a mirror.
Not for reflection.
But for remembering.

Sometimes he gives a shard of the Mirror of the Edge.
A shard that doesn't cut.
It awakens.

Sakura reached the edge.
She sat beside him.
She was silent.
And for the first time – she didn't hold on.

He asked for nothing.
Didn't expect her to pull herself together.

He simply existed –
like silence that doesn't ask you to be strong.

And in that silence,
Sakura felt, for the first time:
she didn't have to prove she was coping.

Being – was already enough.

He handed her a shard.
The light within it trembled.
She looked –
and in the reflection, she didn't see someone broken,
but the one she hadn't called by name for so long.
Not even herself.

It wasn't a miracle.
It was a return.
To herself – before the pain, before the "must," before the silence.

The grass beneath her hand was warm from the sun, slightly damp –
the earth responded with warmth, as if reminding her:

you are not just the one who held on.
You are the one who remained.

Sakura didn't cry.
She simply exhaled deeply –
as if releasing the one she had become
to survive.

The Keeper vanished.
Or perhaps he became her breath –
calm, steady,
in which, at last,
there was space for herself.

Sometimes, to not disappear,
you must see yourself before they taught you
who to be.
And be silent in that silence,
where you finally recognize:
you exist. And that is enough.

Yours, Sakura

Chapter 34. Crystal Deserts
(You Won't Understand It as a Child)

They say in the Crystal Deserts, every true word becomes a crystal.
It pulses with light if it is sincere.
And it cracks if it carries lies, fear, or resentment.
And if it shatters – it can never be put back together.
It disappears.

Sakura didn't know this.
As a child, she thought
this was how everyone lived.

That everyone's mom was like hers.
That all homes were places
where you were heard,
not just listened to.

Her friends adored her mother.
They stayed late.
Shared secrets.
Cried. Laughed.

And they would say:
– "Your mom is so amazing…"

And Sakura thought:
How could it be any different?

Only later,
when she stepped into her own desert,
did she realize:
not everyone's words survive the journey.

Some carry them with pain –
and they crack halfway.
Some wait their whole lives to hear:
"I'm here."
Some never hear:
"I believe in you."

And only then did Sakura understand:
all those years, beside her was a woman
whose words always found their way.
They didn't press. They didn't burn.
They simply – warmed.

As if she had a rare gift –
to speak in a way

that even the fragile
became strong.

In the Crystal Deserts,
it doesn't matter how loud you are.
What matters is whether you carry warmth.

And if your words are alive,
they will reach.
And if you don't know where to start –
just be there.

Sometimes that alone – is already a word.
One that will never shatter.

Yours, Sakura

Chapter 35. The Flower Passage

In this city, there were underground passages by the metro.
Old, worn, smelling of damp.
People climbed up – to their lives, to the light, to their "musts."
But it was in these passages
that sometimes encounters happened,
the kind that seemed accidental,
but stayed in your heart forever.

They were called flower passages.
Because it was there
that time seemed to pause,
and someone would pass light to someone else –
without words.

Sakura walked through one such passage every day on her way to work.
And with her – hundreds of others walked by.
Including him.
A young man who worked with her.
Not closely. But nearby.
They rode the same metro line.

Got off at the same station.
And walked through the same passage.

In the corner, on a small stool,
sat an old woman selling flowers.
Simple ones.
Unfashionable.
Wrapped in cellophane,
as if not for sale,
but as a memory of something warm.

She didn't call out, didn't complain.
She simply sat.
With that quiet stubbornness
of someone who hadn't given up,
even though they could have.

Sakura saw her every day.
And she knew: the young man did too.
They walked the same path.
And one morning, at work,
he approached her –
and handed her a bouquet.

The cellophane was slightly torn.
The flowers – simple, like childhood.

And in that moment
Sakura knew where they came from.

He had bought them from the old woman.
In that very passage.
He didn't say a word.
But she understood everything –
without packaging, without ribbon,
right in her heart.

When Sakura took the bouquet in her hands,
she felt she was holding not just flowers.

In them was kindness.
Awkwardness.
Compassion.
And a great heart
that didn't know how to say, "I love you,"
but tried so hard to be close.

And that's how it began.
With that very bouquet.
With that very morning.
With those simple flowers,
which carried more light
than any bouquet from a fancy store.

In every city, there are passages
where encounters are never accidental.

Someone buys flowers.
Someone gives them.
Someone – understands.

And sometimes, not knowing how to say what matters most,
a person simply hands you a bouquet.
Simple.
Warm.

With an answer you never expected –
but always wanted to hear.

This is how not just a day begins.
But – love.

Yours, Sakura

Chapter 36. How Much of You Remains

In her class, there was a boy. He sat at the last desk in the middle row.
Quiet. Too polite. Almost invisible.
He carried an old briefcase to school – instead of a backpack. Worn, but tidy.
He held it carefully, as if it was something important.
Perhaps a memory. Perhaps protection. Perhaps the only thing he could be proud of.

The class was cruel to him.
Especially the boys.
They laughed. Snatched the briefcase, tossed it around, hid it.
He never complained. Never retaliated.
Just quietly retrieved his things, sat down, and continued.
As if he knew – no one would stand up for him.

One day, Sakura overheard a teacher speaking to another, tiredly, almost in a whisper:

– "In all my years, I've never seen a worse class. No heart. No compassion. Only teeth."

It was terrifying. Because it was true.
And because even she – kind, sensitive, thoughtful – kept her distance.
Just parallel.
She didn't bully him. But she didn't protect him either.
Too afraid to stand out. Or perhaps simply lacking the strength.

But he… he drew.
On the margins of his notebooks – houses, windows, rooftops, bridges.
Thin lines, as if from another world.
A world where no one mocked you. Where you could be yourself.

One day, during a break, when the classroom was almost empty, she approached him for the first time.
Asked quietly:

– "Do you want to be an architect?"

He smiled slightly, without looking up, and answered quickly:

– "I did. But… I'm not one of them."

That phrase stayed with her forever.
"Not one of them."
As if there was a special caste – for whom dreams were allowed. And for everyone else – only watching from afar.

They never saw each other again.
She doesn't know how his life turned out.
But sometimes she thinks of him.
Often – in those moments when she herself is afraid to believe in herself.
When it feels like she won't be enough. Like she doesn't deserve it. Like it's too late.

And every time, she wants to believe that he made it.
That one day he woke up and said, "I am worthy."
That he went to study. Late. From scratch.
That now he builds houses where it's safe to live.
Where everyone has a place.
Even the one who once sat at the last desk and stayed silent while they laughed.

Once, in her notebook, between daily tasks, Sakura wrote a phrase.
Sharp. Accurate. Without sentiment.

You're not afraid of failure.
You're afraid to believe that you deserve more.
That's why you live halfway.

Print it out and hang it on your wall.
Erase it if you want.
But please,
don't live less than you are.

Yours, Sakura

Chapter 37. A Time Capsule: From the Future – to Childhood

If you are reading this – it means you've been through a lot.
You learned to stay silent when it hurt.
You learned to smile, even if a storm raged

inside.
You believed in people – and that was beautiful.
You hoped – simply because you couldn't do otherwise.

When you were betrayed – you searched for the fault within yourself.
When you weren't chosen – you thought you weren't worthy.
When they left – you blamed yourself for not holding on.

But I want you to know:
You are not too much.
You are not difficult.
You are not a mistake.

You are deep. Genuine. Luminous.
And everything within you – matters.
Without conditions. Without "if."

You will learn to live for yourself.
Not because you stopped believing in others.
But because you learned to believe in yourself.

You will become soft – but with boundaries.
You will still feel deeply –

but you will learn to choose who deserves to see it.

You will stop apologizing for your tears.
You will simply start being yourself – calmly, confidently, gently.

And one day, looking at yourself – grown, real – you will quietly say:
"You made it.
You kept your light.
And I am so glad that you – are still you."

Let this message lie deep within.
Like a time capsule.
It will find you exactly when you are ready to hear it.

With love –
Your grown-up Sakura

Chapter 38. A Word You Can Say Only Once
(On truth that sets you free – not to prove, but to finally breathe)

Sometimes you live with a phrase,
one that has never been spoken.
It is like a splinter.
It becomes part of you.
But one day – you decide:
better a wound than silence.

Sakura found this place by accident.
Or so it seemed.

In an alley that wasn't on any map,
a door without a sign.
Only a plaque on the glass:

"Say what you can no longer hold.
Once.
And leave."

Inside – a round room.
A glass dome.
Walls covered with faded inscriptions.
And not a single person.

But the air was thick –
as if thousands of words still hovered there,
unfinished, unsaid.

Sakura stood in the center.
And stayed silent.
For a long time.

She thought about everything
that had piled up in her over the years.

About those who didn't hear her when it
mattered.
About those who demanded she be convenient.
About the words she held back for the sake of
peace.
About the silence she hid behind.

And then she spoke.
Not in a whisper.
And not a shout.
But the way you speak
when you can no longer stay silent.

I am tired of being the one who understands
everything.

Who smooths the edges.
Who stays silent, so others are comfortable.

I no longer want to be strong
if that strength costs me my voice.

I am here.
I feel.
I have the right to be heard.
Even if no one likes
the way I sound.

The words didn't come out like a speech –
but like a release.
Like a stone that had been held in the throat for years.
And finally – was let go.

The room didn't grow quieter.
But inside –
something finally became clear.

Sakura stepped outside.

It was bright.
It seemed like the rain had just ended.

And in her soul – not lightness.
But space.
As if the phrase,
lived aloud,
had freed room for her true self.

Not every word needs to be repeated.
Some live inside for years,
waiting to be spoken once –
and change you forever.

Yours, Sakura

Chapter 39. The True Cost of a Ticket
(Sometimes a voice is worth more than silence)

You can stay silent a hundred times.
Out of politeness.
Out of fear.
Out of "it's not my business."
But one day, a moment comes

when the silence inside becomes so loud
that you can no longer stay silent.

Sakura was fifteen.
An ordinary day, an ordinary trolleybus.
She bought a ticket at the kiosk,
and when she boarded,
she punched it at the nearest validator.
But the stamp barely appeared –
almost invisible.
Sakura went to the next machine and punched it again,
just to be fair.
As she'd been taught.

A few stops later, two inspectors boarded.
Not in uniform – but with badges.
Sharp, rude,
as if they weren't checking tickets –
but looking for guilty faces already.

Sakura showed her ticket and calmly explained
that the first machine hadn't worked.
But they didn't even listen.
– "That's what they all say."

– "It's a fake."
– "Pay the fine. Or come with us."

Their voices were like a wall.
Cold. Unyielding.
And the entire bus – fell silent.
Some lowered their eyes.
Others pretended to look out the window.
Almost everyone stayed silent – not because they didn't see,
but because they were afraid to interfere.
In case they got involved.
In case it was easier to step aside.
As if this had nothing to do with them.

But Sakura noticed something.

They didn't even look at the ticket.
Didn't try to check the date or time.
They didn't need to.

They needed fear.
Confusion.
So that people paid – not because they were guilty,
but because they didn't know what else to do.
They had done this before.

It was a scheme.
Routine. Shameless.
But this time – it didn't work.

Because from the silence, a voice rose.
An old woman in a headscarf – with a bag,
newspapers, and a gaze
that knew how not to be afraid.
She stood up and said loudly:
Sakura had bought a ticket.
She herself had sat next to the validator.
And saw everything.

The inspectors turned on her.
– "Do you want trouble?"
– "We can call the police."
– "Sit down and don't interfere."

The woman didn't sit down.
But her voice trembled.
And Sakura suddenly realized:
if she stayed silent now –
she would be betraying herself.

So, she spoke.

Her voice wasn't loud.
But it was firm.
She explained everything clearly.
No shouting.
No excuses.
The way someone speaks
when they choose – not to stay silent.

The bus fell silent again.
But now it was a pause –
not from fear,
but from the realization:
everyone was listening.

The inspectors left at the next stop.
Irritated.
But they left.

And Sakura remained.

Her heart was racing.
Her knees trembled.
But inside – something had finally fallen into place.
As if she had gained
a new organ – her voice.

Most will stay silent.
Most will look away.
But sometimes one woman,
one girl,
one person,
who says: "Enough" –
is not alone.
It is the beginning.

Yours, Sakura

Chapter 40. A Mirror Without Reflection
(a parable about how one line can reveal everything you fear to see in yourself)

Sometimes you look at yourself – and see nothing.
Because you search for a face.
But only the essence reflects.
And it is not always beautiful.
But it is always true.

Sakura stepped into the library to escape the rain.
It wasn't a new library –
the scent of paper and old wooden shelves
instantly returned her to a place
where you didn't have to rush.

As she wandered between the shelves,
one of the books seemed to lean forward –
a thick volume in a gray cover,
with no title on the spine.
As if it had no name.

Sakura remembered how, as a child, she played a game:
she would pick a page, a line –
as if drawing out an answer to something
she couldn't voice aloud.

She closed her eyes.
Took a breath.
And whispered:
"Page thirty-six... line seven."

She opened it.

It read:

"The one who looks outside – sees form.
The one who looks within – no longer needs a reflection."
(words of Lao Tzu)

And in that moment, something seemed to peel away.
Like a mask not ripped off –
but one that could no longer hold.
There was no pain in it.
Only understanding:
enough of seeking yourself in the eyes of others.

She stepped to a mirror.
The one by the exit – between the shelves,
dim, dusty,
the one that once showed her nothing.

Now it was empty.
And because of that – honest.

Sakura wasn't looking at her face.
She was looking deeper.
And for the first time in a long time,
she didn't care how she looked.
She knew – how she felt.

And in that feeling, there was no image.
But there was presence.
Quiet.
Whole.
Returned.

Sakura stayed in the library,
even though the rain had stopped long ago.
She wasn't in a hurry.
Turned pages – not searching for answers,
but just to hear herself breathe again, alone.
Outside, life continued.
But within – everything had settled into place.

You can search for yourself anywhere:
in another's gaze, in reflections, in approval.
But the true you don't appear when you are seen.
But when you finally
see yourself.

Yours, Sakura

Chapter 41. The Home That Lives Inside

You can miss home a hundred times.
The scent of raspberries.
The window where the sun rose.
But one day you will return –
and realize that everything stayed only within you.
Not outside.

Sakura once spent every summer there.
First – a train ride,
then a long walk.
And every time, when the house appeared around the bend –
something clicked inside her:
she was home.

The lake was a little farther,
always smelling of water and moss.
In the garden grew Chinese cherry,
raspberries, and an old apple tree.
On the second floor – she and her sister.
They slept on the floor, on mattresses, like camping.

And stared out the round window,
where in the mornings, the garden seemed like a picture from a fairy tale.

But many years passed.
The house was sold.
And everything stayed in the past –
or so it seemed.

Until one day, Sakura returned.

The road was the same.
But the grass – taller.
The lake – shallower.
And in place of the apple tree – a neat fence.
The Chinese cherry was gone,
and in its place stood a gazebo.

The house looked almost the same.
But it seemed to gaze past her.
Sakura came closer.
Through a gap in the fence, she saw the window –

the same round one.
And she understood: it felt nothing now.

No pain.
No resentment.
Only emptiness.
As if she had never been there.

And suddenly – calm.

Because everything she loved,
everything that once warmed her,
was not in the walls.
But within her.

And that meant:
she didn't need to enter.
She didn't need to knock.
She had already taken the most important part with her.

You don't have to return to remember.
Sometimes it is enough to come,
stand by the gate –
and feel:
what was once yours – is already within you.
Forever.

Yours, Sakura

Chapter 42. The One Who Doesn't Catch the Ball
(a parable about a staircase that appears only when you walk your own path)

Some steps are invisible at first.
You look ahead – and see nothing.
But the moment you take a step – the path appears.
Not in the world.
But within you.

Sakura hated volleyball.
Not the game itself –
but that moment when the ball was flying,
and everyone's eyes were on you.

She was afraid of the hits.
Got tangled in her own movements.
The ball always landed just out of reach.
The teacher would say, "Focus."
Some classmates rolled their eyes.
And inside, only one thought repeated:
"You're not like them. You're a burden. You're a disgrace."

It was shame,
a shame that stayed in her body –
even after the lesson.
Even at home.
Even at night.

Next was biology class.

Sakura sat by the window, trying to look calm,
though inside she still burned with the sting of failure.
Two girls sat behind her –
the same ones who skillfully smashed the volleyball over the net,
seeming unbreakable.

As everyone pulled out their notebooks,
one of them whispered to her friend:

– "I'm always afraid they'll call me to the board.
Like I won't be able to say a thing.
My heart beats so hard – right in my throat."

The other chuckled lightly:
– "I get panic before any test.
Feels like I forgot everything,
even though I know it all by heart."

They exchanged a glance – and giggled.
Softly. Without drama.

And Sakura froze.

Even them?
Even they were afraid?

In that moment,
something inside her clicked into place.

She wasn't broken.
Her fear just wasn't where theirs was.
And everyone has their own level,
their own ball,
their own board.

After school, she got on her bike again.
Rode for a long time.
And for the first time in ages – she wasn't running away.
She was returning.

And then she thought:

"I don't have to be strong in someone else's game,
if I'm playing my own."

And in that moment,
where there had only been pain before,
there appeared the first step.
Invisible.
But real.

And then – the second.
And the third.

It wasn't a staircase upwards.
Not to someone else's approval.
But to herself.

You don't have to win in someone else's game
to be strong.
Some staircases appear
only when you stop climbing –
and start walking where you can be yourself.

Yours, Sakura

Chapter 43. The Ascendant: The Mirror of Aries
(a parable about the first meeting with yourself)

Sometimes you look in the mirror – and don't see yourself.
You see the familiar shell: the face you wear like a mask.
The voice you use because it's convenient.
The smile – rehearsed. The speech – polished.
But inside, it's like an echo. Or… emptiness.
You don't recognize yourself.

This happened to Sakura.
It was an ordinary morning, when everything was just as always.
But inside – something stirred.
As if someone knocked from within:
"Hey… When was the last time you truly looked at yourself?"

She stepped up to the mirror.
Looked – and froze.
There was something new in the reflection. Or rather – something too forgotten.

Her forehead – stubborn.
Her gaze – with a spark of fire.
Her chin – sharp, like the word "enough."

In this mirror, there was no makeup.
There was Sakura.
The one who had come into this world with a cry of "I am here!",
but who had learned too early to be "convenient," "soft," "quiet."
Not to frighten. Not to disturb. Not to argue.

But now – she couldn't.

That day, she understood:
The Ascendant is not just a degree on a chart.
It is a threshold.
And if you don't cross it – no one will ever truly know you.
Not even you.

Sakura sat on the floor. By the window.
Holding a cup – not because she wanted to drink, but because it made breathing easier.

And in that silence, she heard herself:
– "I don't want to pretend anymore.

– I don't have to be the 'convenient version of myself.'
– I am ready to step out – not with a mask, but with my own face."

Not suddenly, not loudly.
But step out.
And stay.

We spend years wearing a face to fit into the world.
But one day – the world must see our true self.
Even if it's too bright.
Even if it's fiery.
Even if it's not for everyone.
Because only it – is alive.

Yours, Sakura

Chapter 44. A Classmate

In high school, there was a boy Sakura liked.
Longish hair. Black T-shirts.
A voice – rough, confident, calm.
He didn't try to be liked. He simply was –
whole, like the wind.

They weren't friends.
But he spoke to her simply. No pretense. No unnecessary words.
And there was something in him that resonated – not in feelings, but somewhere deeper.
He was one of the first who made her realize the kind of men she felt drawn to.

Later, he dated a bright girl from their class.
Sakura didn't feel jealous.
She simply – looked at him with warmth.
No expectations. No dreams.
Just as someone with whom she felt at ease.

Then – school ended. Ninth grade was the last.
Life split into separate paths.

One day, she saw him on social media.
The same gaze. The same quiet in his eyes.
He was alive. Doing well.
And that alone made her feel a little brighter.

They added each other as friends. Didn't message. Didn't talk.
Just knew, we were there once, together.

And then – she found out he was gone.

He left. Silently. Without warnings. Without goodbyes.

And with him, something else left –
something she thought would always remain.
All that was shared: the bells, the desks, the exams, the school's scents,
the whispers during lessons.
Everything they shared, even without speaking.
Simply being there. Year after year.
And now – gone.

When a classmate dies – you don't just lose a person.
You lose a part of your childhood.

He remained only in old photos.
Where the whole class stood in front of the school.
With a sign. With signatures.
With faces that will never change again.

Yours, Sakura

Chapter 45. Between the Brush and the Heart

When Sakura remembers that girl,
her heart is filled with the scent of watercolor,
the rustle of paper beneath a brush,
and the distant voice of David Bowie.

They studied together.
Completed their practice assignments together.
And in the evenings – they wrote in their journals.
Laughter, notes in the margins,
living thoughts between the lines.

Their friendship was like a painting –
alive, deeper than their age.

That girl lived in a world of colors.
She painted.
Listened to music as if each note carried a message.
Around her, Sakura felt alive.
Brave. A little different – in the best way.

But then – a move.
Sakura left for another country.
They were too young
to understand distance is not the end.

But no one said:
"I miss you."
They were enveloped by silence.
Fragile as glass.
They stayed quiet.
Each in her own home,
with her own longing.

Sakura felt lonely.
She wanted to call so much –
but she was afraid.

Hurt. Unsure how to begin.
And perhaps the other girl felt the same.

Years passed.
They didn't find their way back to each other.
But the memory remained.
Not as a wound. As gratitude.

Because it was with her
that Sakura learned to be herself.
To listen. To dream.
Not to fear being strange or deep.

Sometimes friendship fades not because it ends,
but because words were never found.
And the glass of silence can be shattered –
even by accidental quiet.

Cherish friendship.
Speak while you can.
Sometimes one simple word
saves everything.

Yours, Sakura

Chapter 46. The Distant Voice
(a parable about a voice that finds you, even after years)

Sometimes years pass.
People disappear, familiar routes fade,
and it seems life has gone a completely different way.
You learn to breathe again –
without those who were once part of your air.

And at some point, you are left alone.
Without those who held you. Without words, glances, or shoulders.

And then you stand. Just stand.
And suddenly realize: your spine is not just a bone.
It is an axis. A backbone that holds not just your body, but the sky within you.
When everything collapses – it remains.
Your last, but most honest support.

Sakura was cooking lunch.
An ordinary day, with nothing special expected.

And suddenly – a thought surfaced. Warm, human:
"I wonder how he is? Is he well? What has become of him over the years?"

Once, they studied together,
then worked together.
Shared their daily lives, helped each other, talked after rehearsals,
laughed, were silent, were simply there.
He was a reliable shoulder, an honest gaze, a living voice.
And then – their paths diverged.
For many years.

Sakura wrote:
"Hi, how are you? Can I give you a call?"

The reply:
"Yes, whenever it's convenient for you."

She glanced at the simmering soup and smiled lightly:
"How about now? :)"

And there they were, talking again.
Friends. Simply friends, once connected by life, who still knew how to be warm and genuine.

He told her about a puppy.
How that little bundle with floppy ears became a small daily miracle.
– "My days are brighter with him," he said. "It's like there's always someone to smile at, even in silence."

Sakura smiled, truly happy:
– "A dog is like proof that kindness hasn't gone anywhere.
And loyalty isn't a myth."

And then he suddenly said:
– "You know, I've been thinking… when there's no one around – your spine remains.
It holds you. It remembers how you stood when everything fell apart.
It's your last, but most honest support."

Sakura paused for a second, and there was genuine wonder in her voice:
– "Wow… That's such a philosophical way to put it."

And truly, those words stayed with her.
As if he voiced what she had long felt but never knew how to name.
So simply, calmly – and straight to the heart.

They didn't say goodbye forever.
He said:
– "We'll see each other someday."
She replied:
– "I believe that.
– And let's not lose touch. Even in this big world."
– "Let's not."

The call ended.
But a feeling remained – like coming home.
No pomp. No tears. Just – light.
Just – a person who was once close,
and suddenly was close again.

Because there are connections –
beyond time, beyond distance.
Connections where frequency and location don't matter.
Only one thing matters:
they are alive.
And they are worth keeping.

Yours, Sakura

Chapter 47. A Dream on a Nail Behind the Door

At Sakura's home, behind the door, hung a guitar.
Small, child-sized, with a tiny crack on the body.
It was hung on a nail – like a painting, not an instrument.
Sakura looked at it almost every day.
And thought: one day, I will learn to play it.

On top of the wardrobe, an old accordion gathered dust.
Her grandmother always said that Sakura would learn to play it.
But her dreams were different.
Not a heavy accordion with buttons, but strings, wood, the voice of fingers.

And one day, her dream came true.
A new music school opened.
Her mother took her to enroll.
She remembers that day: the smell of fresh paint, the schedule on the notice board,

and that fluttering excitement in her stomach, like before something important.

Music entered Sakura's life when she was in eighth grade.
Quietly. Confidently.
As if it had been standing outside her door all along, waiting to be let in.

She joined the music school.
Guitar. Strings. Notes. Solfeggio. Choir.
Sounds that had once been just a background suddenly became guides to herself.

Every chord was like a key, unlocking her inner doors.
Every song – a confession.
Every choir rehearsal – a feeling of being part of something big and alive.

For the first time, she heard not only music – but herself.

The strings didn't just play on the guitar – they played within her.
Layers, depths, little cracks she didn't need to hide – but could live through. Sing through.

This is where her poetry began.
This is where her songs began.
This is where she began – her true self.

Years passed. Life sped up, folded in on itself, split into noise and silence.
But the guitar remained.
Sometimes it just stood in the corner. Sometimes – lay under a layer of dust.
But whenever she picked it up – everything returned.

The intonation. The inner voice.
Everything she couldn't express in words but always felt as sound.

Sakura understood:

Music is not about notes.
It is about a connection with yourself.
About the right to be heard – even when you are quiet.
About finding yourself – not through your mind, but through your heart.

And even now, when life becomes too much…
too busy, too loud, too empty,
she takes out the guitar.

Sits down.
Tunes the strings.
And finds the one that plays her soul.

Yours, Sakura

Chapter 48. The Mist No One Saw
(a parable about how one day you stop being –
and start being yourself)

It didn't begin with tragedy.
Not with a loud loss.
Not with betrayal or divorce.
No.

It began with… emptiness.

Sakura couldn't say exactly when it happened.
One day – familiar things stopped feeling real.
Tea became just warm water.
Words no longer clung.
Even her favorite music – sounded as if from underwater.

She kept living.
Got up, as she was supposed to.
Worked, as expected.
Answered, as she had always done.
But inside… it was as if the sound was turned off.

– "I guess I'm just tired," she told herself.
– "It's just autumn. Or hormones. Or lack of sleep. Or just age."

But she didn't tell herself the truth.
Because the truth was terrifying:

She no longer felt like herself.

It felt like her body was still living.
But her soul… had gotten lost somewhere.
Or had moved ahead.
Left a note: "Catch up if you can."

And one morning – she couldn't get up.
Not because she was sick.
But because she saw no point.
Couldn't feel the place where "I" began.

She stepped outside. Just walked.
And found herself in a place she had never seen before.
Even though it seemed she'd lived there a hundred years.
It was a crossroads, covered in mist.
Four roads.
Not a single sign.
Not a single person.
Not a single answer.

And she stopped.
For the first time in her life – not knowing where to go.
And not wanting to pretend she did.

She sank to the ground. Right in the gray dust of the road.
And she cried.
Not from pain.
But from finally letting go.

And in that moment – something happened.
Not a miracle. Not a flash.
But a shift inside.
Quiet, like the turning of a page.
Invisible to the world, but final.

She stood up.
And chose a path.

Not because it seemed right.
But because she suddenly understood she didn't need to find herself.
She needed to be herself.

Sometimes you lose yourself not because you are broken –
but because the old you no longer fit.

You do not disappear.
You simply transform.
And to become yourself,
you must first walk through the mist,
where everything – except the truth – disappears.

Yours, Sakura

Chapter 49. The Diary of Memory
(a parable about a feeling that returns not as a storm – but as a whisper of who you once were)

Many once had a diary with a little lock.
Hidden between books or under a pillow.
Covered with stickers.
With crooked hearts in the margins.
With tiny handwriting,
containing more truth than all spoken words.

The diary knew everything.
Hurt feelings, dreams, crushes.
Fears that no one else was trusted with.
It was like a little chest for the soul –
small, but important.

Sakura wrote in hers too.
In the evenings.
When everyone was busy with their own lives,
she would open her notebook
and it felt like she was speaking to someone
who would never judge.

Sometimes she hid it deeper in the drawer –
as if protecting a part of herself.

And then – she stopped.

She became too busy.
Too serious.
Too grown-up.

Everything that had once been alive
began to feel childish.
Naive.
Unnecessary.

She wrote important things.
Worked.
Spoke correctly.
But inside – something went silent.

One day, sorting through old boxes,
she found her old diary.

The very one.
With the worn cover.
With the faint scent of paper and ink.

She opened it – at random.

And read:

"I don't like that adults make everything so complicated.
I just want things to be real.
To be able to cry if it hurts.
And for it not to be shameful."

Sakura froze.

She didn't remember writing it.
But she knew for sure – it was hers.
The girl who felt too much,
and believed it wasn't a flaw,
but a way of being alive.

She sat there in silence.
As if nothing had happened.
But inside – it was like a window had flown open.
And in that moment, she understood:
what she had been searching for all this time
had never disappeared.
It had just been waiting
for her to stop pretending.

And somewhere deep, without words –
it was as if someone whispered:

"There you are.
I've been waiting for you for so long."

You can forget that you once wrote in lines.
But the lines won't forget you.
They will wait –
and when you return,
they will remind you of who you truly were.

Yours, Sakura

s

Chapter 50. The Circle of Air
(a parable about those whose souls met before words – to be together on Earth)

They say that in one of the warm, high worlds,
on the edge of breath and sky,
there is a place where everything begins with silence.

No wind. No footsteps. No words.
Only a mirror-like lake,

whose reflection shows not a face – but an essence.

Above this lake,
hanging on thin threads of air,
there is an Air Circle.
It does not sway.
It breathes.
And it waits.

Not everyone comes to this circle.
Only those souls whose destinies are intertwined:
not by chance, not temporarily –
but deeply and precisely.
Where one soul becomes light,
and the other responds.

Almost no one knows about such meetings.
They happen long before birth.
Sometimes, only the souls remember.
But it is a great secret.
Too delicate to be told with words.

She didn't know how she got there.
But suddenly she saw –

another soul stood before her.
Small. Strong. Future.

He had not yet been born.
But he already knew that someone important
would be by his side.
Not to save him.
But to be there.
Like light nearby.
Like a hand on the back when learning to walk.
Like silence in which one can breathe freely.

She stood opposite him.
And she also knew:
her light was not for everyone.
But for him – yes.
Not because he couldn't cope.
But because she would be there –
always, when needed.
Quietly. Steadily. Wordlessly.

They did not speak.
They simply stood.
And the silence between them was
not emptiness, but recognition.
Gentle, warm, like a breeze that brings spring.

And then the circle opened.
Beneath them appeared a clear surface –
and from its depths rose
a radiant thread.

It wove, curled,
passed through the heart –
and suddenly flared,
like a name,
remembering itself.

This thread twisted into a symbol.
Not external.
But internal.
Like a flash you see
with your eyes closed,
when you know:
"I will be there. Always."

Later, in another world, in another body,
she would recognize him.
Small.
Newborn.
The son of her friend.
The one who would one day look at her –
and say nothing.

But she would understand.
And he would – too.

Not with words.
Not with memory.
But with the same silence
that existed in the Air Circle.

Sometimes, being a godmother is not a role.
It is a soul that has come by a calling.
A soul that stood in the same circle,
when you didn't yet know how to speak.
But already knew you would need light.
And someone agreed to be it – in silence.

These connections are invisible.
They happen long before Earth.
And if you feel them –
you are one of those who remember.

Yours, Sakura

Chapter 51. A Dress to Grow Into

When Sakura was little, everything seemed slightly faded.
It was a strange time: people started having money, but stores were still almost empty.
Gray windows, identical things, rare glimpses of something real.

She and her grandmother went to the store for butter.
And suddenly – like a flash – there was a dress. Turquoise. With white polka dots.
Impossible, almost fairy-like, standing out among everything else.

Her grandmother took it in her hands – with a joy, as if she had found lost happiness:
– "We will take it. For you to grow into."

Sakura looked at it and felt it wasn't hers. The color was too bright.
But her grandmother glowed.
And when someone you love is happy, you don't want to be the one to dim the light.
Sakura nodded.

She nodded often back then, just so she wouldn't spoil the moment.

The dress was hung in the closet.
It stayed there for a long time, fresh, with a tag, like a promise.
Grandmother would sometimes come in, straighten it, smooth the hem.
As if she was keeping not just fabric – but a dream.

And then Sakura grew up.
The dress finally fit.

But by that summer, everything had changed: stores were full, and choices were real.
For the first time, she could say:
"This is not me. And I have the right not to wear what doesn't feel right."

She never wore that dress.
But she never threw it away either.

Because it wasn't about the fabric.
It was about love.

And Sakura understood:

Sometimes we are given something to grow into.
With love. With hope.
But we grow up – and realize we can choose for ourselves.
And that too – is love.
Not wearing. Not pretending. Being yourself.
And still keeping it.
What was chosen for you – when choice was almost impossible.

Yours, Sakura

Chapter 52. The Valley of Unsent Signs

Sometimes, to understand how you were loved,
you must find yourself in a place
where all the feelings that were never read are kept.

Sakura found herself there one night.
In a dream, or so she thought.
But upon waking – she still remembered the

scent of the air,
in which a longing seemed to float:
"Understand me. Someone, please…"

It was the Valley of Unsent Signs –
a world where acts of love, left unanswered,
gather.
Words that went unheard.
Gifts that seemed unimportant.
Hugs from which someone pulled away.
Silences where someone simply didn't know
how to speak –
but loved.

Sakura walked through the valley.
Strange creatures passed by her –
fragile, shining, cracked, half-whispered.
They did not beg.
They waited,
hoping someone would finally understand what
they meant.

One of them stopped beside her.
It looked like a glowing bundle of light and
paper,

on which something was written.
Sakura leaned closer – and read:

"I didn't know how to speak.
But every time you were hurting,
I silently left tea on the windowsill."

She shivered.
A memory surfaced – a room.
A window.
And a cup that had once seemed random.

Another creature whispered:

"You were upset that I never said I loved you.
But I fixed your computer.
Made sure you had a blanket.
Bought your favorite berries."

Sakura stopped.
Her heart in her throat.
All of it was true.
And she – never understood.

She had always expected words.
While someone had spent their life speaking to
her – with their hands.

She walked on.
And one phrase brushed past her like a shadow:

"You thought I didn't care.
But I just didn't know how to show
that you were the most important thing in my life."

Sakura sank to the ground.
Tears streamed down her cheeks.
She suddenly realized
how much love in her life had gone unnoticed.
Not because it didn't exist.
But because its language was different.

We often seek love in our own language –
and miss those who speak in another.

But if you stop for a moment –
and listen –
you may notice:
you were loved.

Not with words.
But with actions.
With pauses.
A cup of tea.
A warm blanket.
Or a repaired computer.

Yours, Sakura

Chapter 53. When Love Suffocates

When Sakura was twelve, she first understood how painful it could be to become someone's entire world – especially if you never wanted to be.

It was an autumn school camp. Cozy lodges. Crisp air filled with the taste of freedom – a freedom to talk until midnight, to laugh, to fall in love. Almost for real.

There, she met a boy. A boy who seemed to search for someone to cling to, someone to be needed by. And when his gaze settled on her, Sakura couldn't resist. Not because she felt something grand, but because she suddenly craved to be the one someone chose.

At the last dance, he approached her: – Would you like to dance?

Un-break My Heart. Slow dance. A rushed breath. Heart pounding somewhere in her throat.

The next day, on the bus, he asked: – Can I kiss you?

Sakura blushed, shut her eyes tight: – Just on the cheek. And quickly.

He kissed her. She sighed with relief. Thank God. That's it.

But it didn't end.

His class was nearby. He appeared during recess. He called. He praised her. He even told her mother: – Please tell your daughter I love her.

Every. Single. Day.

At first, she was flattered. Then, she grew tired. And then – she began to get angry. Truly angry.

He was everywhere. In her air, in her pauses, in her thoughts. He thought it was love. She thought: Leave me alone. Give me back a little bit of myself.

And at some point – she couldn't take it anymore. She shouted. Harshly. Cruelly. In front of the whole class. Harsher than she intended. But she didn't know any other way.

Later, in class, the door was ajar. And he walked past, eyes red, glancing in. But Sakura didn't look. Couldn't.

She felt ashamed. But she could finally breathe.

That was her first "cruelty." Her first "no." Her first "enough."

And she realized: Sometimes, to stay true to yourself, you have to be the villain in someone else's story. You have to choose yourself. Even if it hurts later. Even if someone cries outside the door.

Yours, Sakura

Chapter 54. The Stone No One Stepped On

Sometimes you end up somewhere you never planned to be. And everything inside protests: "This is a mistake." But in truth – it's a turning point.

The one you truly needed.

Sakura got off at the wrong stop. The bus turned too early, she was distracted, and she missed the button. Nothing dramatic. Just a simple detour.

As she was figuring out her map, she noticed a small newspaper stand. The smell of dust, ink, and something old filled the air – familiar, like childhood during summer breaks.

The vendor, an elderly woman in a knitted beret, helped Sakura find her way, explaining the nearest intersection and how to reach her destination. But before they parted, she added:

"Some people sit on the bench in the little park ahead. The one with the slightly tilted boards. They say there's a special stone beneath it. And something in you changes if you just sit there and think – without rushing, without your phone, just being with yourself."

Sakura smiled, thanked her, and walked on. Yet something inside felt… still. As if a voice whispered: "Go. See for yourself."

She found the bench. Ordinary. But underneath – a stone. At first glance, it seemed plain. But it was warm to the touch. And in its center – a faint line. Like a crack. Like a beginning.

When Sakura touched it, it was as if something clicked inside. As if this day, this accidental turn, was never accidental.

Later, she would remember that stone. And how everything truly began to change from there.

It might be just a bench. Just a random turn. But if something stirs within – it means this is where your life wants to change.

Yours, Sakura

Chapter 55. The Path of the White Wind

They say there are places in this world where you don't step with your feet – but with your memory. You walk, and your heart trembles, as if you are not arriving but returning.

In such a land, no one shouts. They speak with gestures. They do not hug – but they hold space. And the air is such that you suddenly remember that within you is a garden you have not visited in ages.

She came to that place once. Without expectations. Without any thought that it might change something.

But as she stepped onto the narrow street, something within her opened – not like a door, but like the eye of the soul.

"I know this," she thought. "I've never been here. But I know this."

And for the first time in her life, a thought came to her that wasn't just a thought, but a knowing:

If souls could come to this Earth more than once, mine would have begun its journey here.

From that day, everything changed.

Not in her passport. Not in her affairs. But in her sense of knowing: now I know – I have found it. What I never sought in words. What always lived in me – but had no shape.

There are places where you do not find yourself – you remember. You remember who you were long before you became a name, a role, a title, or a fear.

The Path of the White Wind – is not a road to a country. It is a road to yourself. To the you who remembers where she first came from.

Yours, Sakura

Chapter 56. The Parable of the Comet and the Cornfield

When Sakura was little, in one rare year, a comet approached Earth. Its name has long faded from memory – but the feeling remains. It was as if the Universe itself had come closer, visible, breathing. The comet could be seen with the naked eye, and everyone talked about it. People searched for a place away from city lights, where the sky was open and true.

Sakura's neighbor, a man with a kind voice and an eager gaze, said: – Tonight, it will be visible. It will pass slowly, with a tail – like burning silence. A once-in-a-lifetime sight. We must see it.

Sakura went with her mother. The neighbor stepped out with his wife and son – the boy carefully carrying a tripod, as if he were entrusted with a piece of the sky.

They walked along the familiar path behind the house, where there used to be a field. Where now there are houses and glowing windows, there once grew corn. Tall, rustling, smelling of warm earth and sweet green leaves. The paths through it were narrow, warm, like a palm you remember even in dreams.

And above it all stretched the sky. Deep, dark, untouched by streetlights, pure as a bowl where night had settled.

They set up the telescope. They waited. No one spoke. Not even the children. It was as if each one felt – this was not just watching. This was a meeting.

And then – it appeared. Not suddenly, not like a flash. Slowly. As if a secret fold in the sky opened, and light slipped out. Thin, alive, with a fiery trail, stretching behind it like breath.

Sakura looked through the telescope, then just looked up. The comet drifted through the darkness, and time seemed to turn transparent.

The boy, the neighbor's son, whispered: – I thought it would just be a light... He paused. – But it feels like... it's looking back.

Years passed. That field is gone – built over. The paths where corn once rustled are now paved. The sky, once a dome overhead, hides behind rooftops. People rush. Staring at screens. Almost no one looks up.

But Sakura grew up. Now she lives on another continent. A completely different life. With other streets, faces, language. But sometimes – in the evenings – she still looks up.

The sky here is different. The moon is the same, but it seems slightly turned. Like a person you were once close to, now greeting you with a reserved nod. As if it, too, senses the distance between you. Not just in kilometers.

And in such evenings, in this slightly slanted moonlight, something within her suddenly opens – like a forgotten door. And everything returns. The smell of warm earth. The narrow paths through tall stalks. The voices nearby. And the comet – thin, alive, like a breath of the heavens. And someone's voice beside her. – I thought it would just be a light... – But it feels like... it's looking back.

Not everything in life needs to be repeated. Sometimes – one moment is enough. One glance at the sky. One comet. One feeling that stays with you forever.

Don't miss your comets. Even if you have to walk in the dark for them. Even if they pass by in just a few minutes.

Because it is moments like these – that make us alive.

Yours, Sakura

Chapter 57. The Girl Who Followed the Sound of Music

Everything began with a cabbage pie and a fresh poster on the wall by the entrance.

Cabbage pies always sold out first – the most delicious. And that day, Sakura managed to get one.

The man behind the counter – the one who knew who loved cherry and who preferred apple – handed her the warm, homey pie, gestured toward the new poster at the door, and said: – They say it's a good band. I listened. Your kind?

Sakura looked up – and her heart answered with a line she knew by heart: "Our little flock is flying into the sky."

And everything within her stirred. As if someone quietly called her by name. I must be there.

That song once saved her. In that winter without light, she listened to it in her headphones, and it felt like a hand touched her shoulder. This isn't just a band. This is her flock.

The festival was in another city. She wrote down the stop, the route, checked everything. Got on the bus. Made it. But when she stepped out – she found herself on a bridge.

Her bag weighed on her shoulder. The music was faint, an echo – as if someone played it beyond the world.

She walked down, reached the river, a small beach. Looked around. Listened. But the festival wasn't there.

She went back. Walked along the road. Cried. From confusion, from exhaustion, from that strange pain when you almost reached – but missed.

Yours, Sakura

Chapter 58. Sakura and the Strawberry

Sakura was sitting on a bench in the shopping mall.
She had a cup of jasmine tea, warm hands, and a little time –
her daughter had gone to try on a dress.

She simply sat, watching.
She loved catching these moments – when you didn't have to do anything.
When the world moved past you,
and you – you were in that quiet pause between breaths.

And then she saw it:
a man with an expensive ice cream,
beautiful, glazed with pink icing and decorated
with chocolate-covered strawberries.

One of the strawberries slipped off.
It fell to the floor.
He noticed.
But he didn't bend down.
He didn't pick it up.
He just walked away.
Clean, confident, with an expression that said,
"Not my problem."

Sakura took a sip of her tea.
And the strawberry remained.

At first, people stepped around it.
Then someone kicked it.
It rolled across the hallway – back and forth,
like an unwanted ball.
The chocolate turned dull,
the berry – sticky, dirty.

And everyone who kicked it
wore ties, carried branded bags, walked with
straight backs.

But their eyes held no light.
Only emptiness and a habit of not noticing.

Sakura watched – and suddenly she felt
that it wasn't just a strawberry.
It was something lost. Foreign. But familiar.
Like someone's feeling left behind.
Like a care trampled underfoot.
Like tenderness ignored because no one had time for it.

And then – one little girl.
Small, in simple clothes.
She stopped.
Bent down.
Picked up the strawberry with a napkin and threw it away.
Quietly. Without fuss.
With dignity.

Sakura smiled.

Sometimes it's the quiet ones,
those who don't shine, who don't throw dust in your eyes,
who are the only ones who remember:

what is made with love should never be trampled.

We've dropped too much – and keep walking, thinking others will clean up after us.
But indifference – it sticks. It spreads. It comes back.

Yours, Sakura

Chapter 59. When Love is Wrapped in a Gift

Sometimes love speaks loudest in a silent gesture.

It was their first New Year together.
Not just a date on the calendar, but the first small bridge between "I" and "we."
The first holiday when Sakura could put into a gift everything she felt – but didn't yet know how to say aloud.

He had an old backpack.
Simple, sturdy, reliable – the kind of thing he always chose for himself: meant to last, without unnecessary shine.
He knew how to value what he had, to care for things as he cared for everything important in his life.
He was humble, careful, and genuine – her beloved man, in whom she saw far more than he ever saw in himself.

Sakura couldn't explain it with words.
She just knew for their first holiday he deserved something different.
Something that would tell him – without grand speeches:
"You deserve the best. And you can accept it."

She received one of her first paychecks –
and almost immediately, without hesitation, she went to the shopping center.

There, among the shimmering displays and the sound of festive music, she searched.
She unzipped bags, touched the fabric, checked the seams – as if she wasn't looking for just a

backpack,
but for something more: not a thing, but a talisman.

And when she found it – she knew instantly.
This backpack was strong, like his character, and beautiful in its simplicity.
Just like he deserved to be seen.

The price was high.
More than half of her monthly salary.

For her, it was almost an unaffordable gift.
So expensive that reason whispered to stop.
But her heart said something else:
"The one you love deserves the best – even if it means reaching a little beyond your means."

She stood at the checkout, holding the box, her fingers trembling slightly.
Not from doubt.
But from the sense of doing something important.

When her card touched the terminal, Sakura felt truly grown-up for the first time – not because

she could buy something,
but because she could give love.

On New Year's Eve, under the glow of their first
Christmas tree, decorated with old ornaments
and the warm light of garlands,
she held the box, and her heart raced unevenly.

What if he gets upset?
What if he thinks it's too much?
What if she can't say everything she feels
through this gift?

But then she thought quietly:
"I'm not giving him a thing. I'm giving him the
belief that he deserves to be happy."

And she stepped forward.

She handed him the box.

He untied the ribbon, lifted the lid –
and a storm of emotions swept across his face:
surprise, confusion, a touch of anxiety.

"This is… too much," he whispered, almost
shyly.

He never knew how to accept expensive gifts.
Not because he didn't dream,
but because he was taught to cherish little and
take care of what he had.

He took the backpack in his hands – slowly, like
something precious.
He touched the leather, the zippers, the straps –
with that awkward tenderness
that only those who suddenly receive more than
they ever thought possible feel.

And in his fingers, there was something that
pierced Sakura's heart:
a mix of joy, humility, and childlike wonder.

He used that backpack for years.
He took care of it, repaired it, cleaned off the
dust.
But more importantly – he carried within him
that day, that box, that faith in him
that someone once wrapped in a gift.

And perhaps it was with that backpack that their
real family began –
where things became more than just things.

She didn't want to give him a backpack.
She wanted to give him the belief that he deserved the very best.

Because sometimes the most precious gifts are not things,
but feelings hidden between stitches, the scent of leather, and trembling hands.

Yours, Sakura

Chapter 60. An Envelope with a Personal Meaning

Sometimes the most meaningful gifts don't arrive amid the noise of celebrations,
but in the quiet where you can hear a dream's heartbeat.

Once, while watching TV, Sakura accidentally caught a glimpse of a musical – "Juno and Avos."

Just a few minutes – but it was enough for something inside her to change forever.
Every note, every sound seemed to touch the most delicate string of her soul.

It was a love story – not a fantasy, not something glittering, but something real.
And the voice.
That unforgettable voice of the actor she knew and admired from movies – strong, deep, with a beautiful rasp,
as if each note carried the weight of a lived life.
He didn't just sing – he lived every word, pouring a piece of his soul into each one.

Sakura dreamed of seeing that musical live.
But the dream seemed almost impossible: the tickets were expensive, and in their family, money always went toward more necessary things.

She never asked.
Only once, during a family dinner, she let her wish slip – so quietly that she barely noticed herself saying it.

Her stepfather heard.

He took on extra work.
A bit more money, one more evening of effort –
and one evening, he simply handed her an envelope,
as if offering her a piece of light.

"This is for you," he said, almost casually.

Inside was a ticket.
A real one.
To that very theater.

Sakura stared at the thin paper with golden lettering and suddenly felt a warm wave of tears rising in her throat.
She was afraid to breathe – afraid to shatter this fragile happiness that had suddenly become real.

But the path to a dream is rarely straightforward.

On the day of the performance, disaster struck: the actor she so admired broke his leg.
The show was postponed for two months.

Those two months felt like an eternity.
The ticket lay between the pages of a book – and every time she opened it, Sakura remembered: dreams know how to wait.

And finally, the day came.

Sakura prepared carefully.
She chose her best outfit – a light dress she had saved for a special occasion.
She slipped on heels – and as she walked along the cobbled streets toward the theater, the delicate click of her steps, uncertain, almost in time with her own heartbeat, echoed in the cool spring air.

Before entering, she stopped by a tiny flower shop and bought a bouquet – modest but chosen with such care
as if each stem knew who it was meant for.

And then she was there, sitting in the darkened hall, breathing in the scent of dusty curtains and old wood.
The bouquet rested on her lap, her heart racing like it was waiting for a miracle.

And when the first notes sounded, when voices soared beneath the theater's high arches, her heart ached with joy.

She lost track of time.
It was as if she lived through the characters' pain, their love, their hopes.
Every song brought tears to her eyes, and she made no effort to hold them back.

At the finale, the entire hall rose.
People clapped, standing, for a long time – as if afraid to let go of this miracle.

Next to her stood a woman – a stranger, but in that moment, someone incredibly familiar.
Their eyes were full of tears.
They smiled through them, clapping, feeling the same thing in their chests: gratitude for the beauty of dreams that sometimes come true so quietly, so gently, so unexpectedly.

And Sakura knew: this moment would stay with her for the rest of her life,
one of those moments that shine within you, even when everything around seems dark.

Sometimes the biggest dreams come true without fanfare.
They quietly enter your heart – through the trembling paper of a ticket, through the warm

gaze of someone who heard your wish, even if you almost didn't say it aloud.

True miracles are made by people.
Without magic, without promises.
Simply because love knows how to hear even the softest dreams.

And then a dream doesn't arrive in a golden carriage.
It comes in the whisper of an old theater hall, in tears on the cheeks of strangers nearby,
in the standing ovation that sounds louder than any music.

And it stays alive within you – forever.

Yours, Sakura

Chapter 61. When Someone Sees More Than Just the Crowd

Sometimes an ordinary day becomes the first celebration of believing in yourself.

It was just another ordinary day in the life of students.
A one-day side job – not much money,
but back then, even a drop of one's own earnings felt like an ocean of freedom.

Sakura and her friend had signed up with a company that helped students find such gigs.
This time, it was a crowd scene for an advertisement for a well-known mobile operator.
The theme – football.
The location – a real stadium.

On the field, "players" were running – extras dressed in team uniforms.
And the stands were filled with "fans" – other students painted in bright brand colors.
Someone painted a makeshift flag on Sakura's cheek, handed her a drum, and told her:
"Cheer! Be happy! Live the moment!"

But she didn't pretend.

She beat the drum with all her heart,
she shouted, she clapped, she cheered,
as if her team was truly fighting for victory.

In the crowd, where everyone was playing a part,
Sakura was truly alive.

At first, no one paid attention.
The cameras filmed wide shots – waves of cheering fans, a sea of faces.

But then something changed.

The director stopped the take.
His gaze swept across the stands.
And suddenly, aloud, he said:

– The girl with the drum.
Let's get her in close-up.

Sakura froze.
Her.
All of this was now about her.

Assistants guided her closer to the cameras.
The lights grew brighter, the lens zoomed in.

And she began to beat the drum again,
but now her fingers trembled slightly –
not from fear,
but from a quiet, blossoming joy.

They filmed several takes.
Laughter, applause from the crew.
And the news: the pay for a close-up was double.

But the most valuable thing that day wasn't the
money in an envelope.

The most valuable thing was the feeling:
someone had noticed her effort.
Someone saw her life in that small drum.

It was her first little, quiet triumph.
A victory that wouldn't be recorded in any
diploma, nor printed in any newspaper.
But one that would remain forever in her heart.

Sometimes an ordinary day
becomes the first milestone on the path to your
true self.

Where you truly live –
not just wave a flag in your hand.

Whatever you do, do it as if the world depends on you.
Even if you're just a girl with a drum in the crowd.

Because one day, someone will see it too:
that within you – there is more than a crowd.

Within you – there is life.

Yours, Sakura

Chapter 62. When Strict Eyes Hide Quiet Support

Sometimes a single encounter becomes an answer to a question you were too afraid to ask yourself.

Some people enter a room – and it instantly becomes quieter.
Not because they are loud.

But because their presence is a reminder: before you stand dignity.

Such was the case with the Pharmacology Instructor.

A woman with a posture sculpted out of light, with a walk so graceful it seemed she didn't walk – she glided.
Always impeccably dressed, with flawless makeup, neatly styled hair,
but most of all, with an inner strength that was impossible to mistake or ignore.

When Sakura entered her senior year of college and learned that it would be this instructor who would teach Pharmacology,
a flicker of anxiety stirred within her.

Rumors surrounded this woman:
strict, demanding, unforgiving of negligence.

And they turned out to be true.

On the first day of class, Sakura sat at the front – on a small metal chair that seemed to tremble with her nerves, its legs slightly rattling in sync with her own heartbeat.

She was genuinely afraid.
Not of the person – but of the standard this woman set simply by being there.

But the lessons went on.
And along with them, something inside Sakura began to change.

Pharmacology was complex, but it came alive in her classes.
She didn't read from a textbook.
She spoke as if the substances, molecules, and medications were living beings,
and even those who feared chemistry found themselves listening, breath held.

Fear gradually melted away.
In its place, another feeling emerged –
respect.
Deep, genuine respect.

Sakura pushed herself.
Gave her all.
Not out of fear anymore –

but out of a desire to be worthy of the high
standard set before her.

She spent nights over her notes, memorizing the
mechanisms of drug actions,
learning the interactions of substances.
Not for the grade.
But because, for the first time in her life, she
wanted to meet the mark.

And then, without warning,
the Instructor called a meeting of the faculty
council.
Department heads. A commission.

She did not invite Sakura.

At that meeting, she raised a question:
a student who works this hard should not have to
pay for her education.

A few days later, the Instructor approached
Sakura in the hallway.

Poised, composed – but there was more in her
eyes than mere duty.

– You are being transferred to a scholarship program, – she said quietly.
– You've earned it.
And then, a little softer, with warmth in her voice:
– Keep studying well.
You are capable of more than you think.

She lingered for a moment –
as if wanting to say something else,
but trusted her words to carry enough.

And then she walked away.

No grand speeches.
No applause.

Leaving behind a feeling in Sakura's heart –
that the greatest recognition doesn't come in diplomas or medals,
but in the silent faith someone places in you.

But Sakura's life was not just about victories.

There was a time when youthful idealism clouded her soul with heavy storms.
Everything seemed wrong.
Nothing made sense – not in studies, not in

thoughts, not in life.
The weight pressed from all sides.

And one day, during a lesson, sitting in the front row,
Sakura didn't even notice when a thin, nearly invisible tear silently traced down her cheek.

The Pharmacology Instructor saw everything.

She did not scold.
Did not question.
Only, as she passed by, she whispered – so only Sakura could hear:

– Come to my office. We need to discuss something.

And she calmly continued the lesson.

For the other students, she assigned tasks: to review their notes, prepare materials – to keep them busy.

Then she left for her office.
And Sakura followed.

For nearly the entire class, they talked.

Behind that closed door, the Instructor was no longer just a teacher.
She became a Mentor.

A person who saw beyond grades.
A person who sensed the heart, even when it was silent.

And she spoke.

She spoke in a way that made the weight lighter. She spoke in a way that, deep inside, reignited a small but genuine spark of confidence in Sakura: "I will be okay."

That conversation stayed with Sakura for life.
Not the tests, not the grades.
But that one hour of understanding and quiet strength.

Sometimes, behind a strict gaze, hides a warm hand ready to support you in your darkest moment.

Sometimes the most important thing we receive in life is not knowledge.
But faith.

The quiet faith of those who see more in us than we see in ourselves.

And that faith becomes the bridge by which we one day cross the darkest river of our life –
to where true strength begins.

Yours, Sakura

Chapter 63. When Pain Teaches Us to Love Even More

Sometimes the most important journeys begin not with plans – but with a quiet, childhood promise.

The puppy was tiny – almost weightless.
A fluffy bundle of joy, barely two months old.

He had the most trusting eyes in the world,
a little wet nose, and an endearing attempt at barking,
as if he wasn't entirely sure of his own voice yet.

Sakura was just a child – eight or nine years old.
And for the first time in her life, she felt the pure, unfiltered happiness
that comes with holding a life in your hands.

She cared for him, fed him, played with him, tucked him in at night.
And the puppy, in return, loved her with all his tiny heart.

It seemed like nothing bad could exist in a world where such love was possible.

But a few months later, the puppy fell ill.

At first, it was just a slight weakness.
But it quickly turned into a severe condition, worsening with each passing day.

The veterinarian was far – nearly an hour's walk from their home.
And every day, Sakura and her mother made that journey,
through rain, wind, and exhaustion – carrying the puppy in their arms.

They gave him injections, followed the treatment,
did everything they could to help him fight.

But the illness proved stronger.

Not all small creatures can endure such battles.
And one day, the struggle ended.

The puppy was gone.

It was the first real heartbreak of Sakura's life.

There, on the doorstep of their home, holding an empty collar in her hands,
she made herself a promise.

Not for show.
Not out loud.

A promise to always be there for those who couldn't protect themselves.

"I will grow up and become someone who helps little hearts fight for life."

The years passed.

School. Studies. Exams.

When the time came to choose her path, Sakura didn't hesitate.

She chose the road that had begun that day –
not out of ambition, not out of a dream,
but from a simple, quiet resolve:
to be there where it was most needed.

And one day, while taking her entrance exams,
she felt it – she was fulfilling the promise she made to herself that day,
hugging her puppy for the last time.

And in that choice, there were no grand words, no pride.

Only a warm, gentle silence in her heart.
A silence of loyalty.

The strongest paths begin when a small hand clutches an empty collar –
and a heart makes a promise to be there.

Not to be a hero.
Not to become someone great.

But simply to one day save a little life.
And in doing so, save something within yourself.

Yours, Sakura

Chapter 64. When the Silence of the Stage Becomes Yours

Some moments never become loud in the world — but they remain loud within us forever.

They say that the stage loves the strong.

But Sakura knew:
the stage doesn't hear strength.
The stage hears honesty.

And sometimes honesty speaks not louder than a whisper.
Sometimes with trembling hands.
Sometimes in a voice barely above a murmur.

But it is precisely in those moments, when you are genuine,
that the world becomes a little quieter,
just to listen to you.

For her, the guitar was always more than just music.
It was salvation.
A conversation without words.
A thread connecting her to the world,

one she could hold onto even when everything
else was falling apart.

She studied at a music school,
performed at concerts,
learned how to stand before an audience.

But this time was different.

This time, Sakura wasn't bringing scales or
rehearsed melodies to the stage –
she was bringing herself.

A song she had written.
A song where her silence lived.
Her pain.
Her light.

"Holosiivska Spring."

A festival for young voices.
For those who dared to sing not someone else's
truth, but their own.

When the college announced the competition,
Sakura hesitated for a long time.

What if no one listened?
What if she made a mistake?

What if her voice faltered?
What if her fingers slipped on the strings?

And yet – she applied.

At the auditions, she sat on a high stool.
The guitar felt warm in her hands –
but her fingers were almost numb from anxiety.

The world wavered before her eyes.
Her heart pounded somewhere in her throat.

Another moment – and she might have run.
But she stayed.

And she sang.

The first chords were quiet, almost hesitant.
Her voice wavered at the beginning,
as if the song itself was afraid to escape.

But the longer she played,
the deeper she immersed herself in the melody,
the stronger her voice became.

On the most precious lines –
where all her truth lived –
it rang out true.

And in that song, she finally found herself.

She was chosen.

On the stage of the capital's main university,
everything was real.

Bright spotlights.
A dark hall.
The rustling of hundreds of strangers.

The guitar trembled in her hands.
Her fingers feared missing the strings.

But when she struck the first chord –
the silence of the hall suddenly became warm.
Not frightening – but alive.

And Sakura sang.

At first, softly, cautiously.
But with each line, each word,
fear retreated.

And by the end, she wasn't just a timid girl anymore –
she was a person who, for the first time,
allowed her heart to sing out loud.

The applause didn't come immediately.

First, there was a moment of silence –
piercing, drawn out.
And then the hall filled with clapping.

Warm.
Sincere.

And in that applause,
Sakura heard the most important thing:
she had been heard.

Not because she was flawless.
But because she was real.

The deepest stages of our lives often unfold
without loud fanfare.

Sometimes we step out into the world with
trembling hands,
a voice that seems about to break,
a heart that feels too fragile.

But it is in those moments –
when we decide not to hide ourselves –
that the world grows quieter.

And it listens.

And we realize:
to be heard,
you don't need to be perfect.
You need to be alive.

Yours, Sakura

Chapter 65. The Star at the Desk

He appeared in their school at the beginning of their final year.
When everything was already settled –
who had what reputation,
who was friends with whom,
who sat where,
and who it was best not to fall in love with,
just to avoid complicating an already tense spring.

He didn't just arrive – he entered like stepping onto a stage.
Tall, fair-haired, with a face resembling that of a

singer who had been a teenage idol five years ago.
He didn't simply walk in – he filled the air around him.

First, the girls in their class sighed.
Then – the ones from the parallel classes.
And soon – even the seniors.

They would pop into Sakura's classroom under all sorts of pretexts:
to borrow chalk, return a notebook, clarify something.
Some didn't even bother with excuses – they just came to "visit" their friends,
hoping to stand by the wall, exchange a few words with him,
catch his glance.

His arrival became an event.
The atmosphere in the classroom changed.
Echoing, heightened, like the moments before a school dance.

But Sakura just watched.
Not with admiration.

With a detached attention.
As if listening to music that wasn't to her taste.

Everything about him seemed too polished:
his gestures, his gaze, his intonation.
He knew exactly when to laugh, when to fix his hair,
and how to look into someone's eyes so that the girls would remember it for hours.

But to Sakura, there were other notes beneath it.
Too rehearsed.
Too superficial.

One day, she saw him brush past a younger girl in the hallway,
deliberately bumping her shoulder.
He didn't apologize.
He didn't even look back.
He just smirked, as if checking off a box.

And then, like a blow to the chest:
they seated him next to her.
At the same desk.

– I'm here now, – he smiled. – Get used to it.

She said nothing.
Something clenched inside her.
He wasn't just a guest in their class anymore.
Now, he was in her space.

He began his game.
Jokes.
Notes.
Comments scribbled in the margins of her notebook:
"You're strange. That's intriguing."

And she stayed silent.
She tore out the pages.
Switched covers.
Built a wall of silence.

He tried to get her attention.
She refused to respond.
He was used to being adored.
She knew how not to love pretense.

And then one day, when he interrupted the teacher once again,
stealing the class's attention,
Sakura calmly stood up.

She picked up her textbook.
And struck him lightly on the head.

Not out of rage.
But like someone switching off a too-loud TV.

She sat back down.
And continued writing.

He didn't bother her again.

A few days later, he approached her during break:
– You're strange.

She nodded.
– Thank you.

There are people who enter a room, and everyone seems to hold their breath.
They fill the space around them as if they fear it might swallow them whole.
They collect glances, capture sighs,
hoard confessions that no one dares to say aloud.

They drive others mad.
They seem like a dream – until you look for more than five seconds.

And then you see it all:
Every gesture – rehearsed.
Every smile – part of a strategy.
And the emptiness beside them –
once you stop being enchanted.

Sometimes only one person in the crowd doesn't
freeze before a star.
And that person – is a mirror.
They don't clap.
They see who you have become,
and who you stopped being a long time ago.

If you are lucky enough to meet such a person –
don't be angry.
They're not here to break you.
They're here to bring you back.

Yours, Sakura

Chapter 66. The Minute and the Notebook

Sometimes a small notebook is worth more than
a treasure map.

Sakura always believed in the magic of sound.
She knew that a voice could be a key –
to doors, to hearts, to dreams.

In those days, phones were different.
They didn't lie in your pocket, didn't answer by themselves.
Every number was like a secret passage –
you had to obtain it, earn it, ask for it… or lure it out.

One spring morning, when the city was just beginning to bathe in April light,
Sakura and her friend sat on the floor among old records and cassettes.
They listened to a band that smelled like the sea and sounded like goodbyes,
discussed lyrics, plucked at guitar strings.

And then – as if fate itself had winked –
one of their acquaintances, a violinist from a local art group, let something slip.
He had the phone number of a musician with storm-grey eyes –
the guitarist of that very band.

And not just any number.
His home number.

– We're not going to call, are we? – her friend asked, hiding a smile behind a mug of cocoa.

– Of course not, – Sakura replied.
And then they got up, put on their jackets, and walked to the nearest payphone.

They were shaking.
But not from the cold.
From anticipation.
From the strange thrill of attempting the impossible.

– Hello?
– Good evening… Sorry to bother you… This is Sakura and her friend.

He answered.
The musician with storm-grey eyes.
The one.
His voice was warm, real, alive.
And, surprisingly, not annoyed.

They talked about music.
And then, gathering a fresh burst of courage, Sakura asked:

– We know you are friends with the one whose songs sound like freedom –
not as a slogan, but as a friend's voice.

The singer of that band, where every word felt
like stepping on cobblestones,
and every chorus – like a cry of freedom.
Do you happen to have his number?

There was a pause.
Then he smiled, even over the phone:
– Call back tomorrow. I'll find it and give it to
you.

Perhaps, in his answer, there was a touch of
hesitation,
a slight disbelief that these girls would remember
and call again.

But they did.

Only this time, his wife answered.

– Pasha isn't here, – she said.
– But he promised us… – her friend's voice
wavered, almost in tears.

And then something magical happened.
The woman paused.
And then she said:

– If he promised, then it will be.
Wait a minute, I'll get the notebook.

That minute felt like an eternity.
They stared at each other, holding their breath,
afraid that even a loud inhale could shatter this
fragile possibility.

But then the woman returned.
Her voice was calm, like a quiet window with
white curtains.
And she began reading the number aloud.

Their fingers trembled, scribbling it on a scrap of
paper,
there in the cold phone booth,
as if writing down the coordinates to the stars.

They didn't call immediately.
Too sacred. Too surreal.

But that number, written in trembling letters,
wasn't just a contact – it was a bridge.
A reminder that the world wasn't so closed if
you asked with kindness.

The world always answers those who dare.
But it answers even more warmly to those who

keep kindness in their hearts – even when asking for the impossible.

Because sometimes the most important thing isn't who you reached,
but what voice you spoke with.

And if your voice is not demand, not insistence, but a timid, sincere "hello," –
doors will open.
Sometimes, even the ones locked tight.

Yours, Sakura

Chapter 67. The Only Ice

Some lessons last only an hour. But they change you forever.

When Sakura was still just a little girl, her parents had long been living apart.
Different keys, different routes, different conversations in kitchens where shared laughter

had become a distant memory.
She didn't complain. She simply lived. And she dreamed.

Figure skating had been her love long before she ever touched the ice.
Every Olympic broadcast, every championship, every performance on TV – Sakura would freeze in place, mesmerized.
She could spend hours watching the skaters spin, the blades gliding over the ice.
In her room, she would mimic their movements, turning on her toes, listening to the music as if it were a language only she could understand.

Her dream wasn't just beautiful – it was alive.
And her mother knew it.
She saw how Sakura's eyes lit up when she watched the screen, how hope danced in her small body.
And one day, her mother said:

– I can take you to figure skating lessons.

Sakura froze. It was like a beam of light after a long darkness.
Like hearing "yes" in a world that more often

whispered "no."
A joy so sharp it almost hurt, as if she couldn't fully believe it.

They packed up. They had to travel to a neighboring city.
But that didn't scare her.
When you are headed towards a dream, even a foreign city feels like home.

The ice rink was enormous, with walls of glass reflecting the frosty February air.
The instructor was strict, reserved, but kind.
He showed her how to lace up her skates.

The skates were white, new. To her, they seemed incapable of failure – only flight.

Sakura stepped onto the ice.
It was cold, alive, slippery, and accepting.
As if the whole rink knew this was her first step – and allowed it to happen.

She moved, shaky but determined.
And for the first time in her life, she felt herself inside a dream.

Not outside, not watching from the back row –
but right in the heart of the moment.

She thought:
"Now I'll have my own class. Now I'm just like those girls in dresses, with their perfect hair, with their mothers cheering in the stands…"

But it wasn't a class.
It was a single lesson.

Her parents couldn't agree.
Her father – couldn't make it.
Her mother – grew tired.
A week passed. Then another.
And soon it felt like it was too late to return.

And no one noticed how her one and only ice melted away.

She never went back to that rink.
Though she returned to that city many times –
for other reasons, other errands.
Sometimes she would pass by the ice palace, stealing a glance at its glass walls.
But she never went inside.
And the skates stayed in the closet – a silent

reminder that not everything you love can become yours.

Along with them stayed a feeling – like she had once stepped into a fairy tale, only to be cut out of the scene.

Most painfully – no one apologized.
No one said, "We understand how much this meant to you."
No one hugged her. And she never asked.
Because children often stay silent.
They think maybe it's their fault.

Years went by.

Sakura remembered everything: the crisp sound of the ice, the scent of the locker room, the chill on her cheeks.
It wasn't just a memory – it was a capsule of pain.
Quiet. Icy. Real.

But with time, she learned to open that capsule not with bitterness – but with respect.

Because it was this unfulfilled dream that became fuel.

It was this disappointment that later made her refuse to give up,
to never leave someone halfway,
to stand by those whose skates trembled at their first step.

Sometimes the greatest childhood pain is not a wound but a lesson you promise never to repeat.
And if you carry that pain carefully, without letting it poison you – it becomes a compass.
It teaches you to be the adult who stays.
Who supports.
Who arrives.

The world doesn't owe us second chances.
But it waits for us to become the ones who create them for others.

And if you were given just one chance on the ice – hold on to how it felt to step onto it.
And when someone else stands at the edge, their hands trembling – you will be there.
Because now you know what it's like to skate just once and wait a lifetime.

Yours, Sakura

Chapter 68. The Radio-tower and the Stars

Sometimes you glance at something – and someone beside you turns it into a journey.

Some evenings were never meant to follow a straight path.
They were made to drift – to lead you away, toward something unexpected but deeply yours.

That evening, Sakura was in an especially good mood.
Not for any reason – just a quiet joy bubbling from within.
She wanted to walk, to breathe, to feel the world stretch a bit wider than usual.
She stepped off the evening train, a smile lingering on her lips, as if it had a life of its own.

The day didn't want to end – and neither did she.

He walked a little behind her. Then alongside her.
Sakura noticed him back on the train – a look that carried no intention, but perhaps a hint of curiosity.

He didn't speak first. He just walked nearby.
And she sensed it: he also wanted this encounter but didn't dare begin it.

She turned to him, her voice light as if making a simple observation:

– Does it seem like we're headed the same way?

He smiled, a little relieved.

– Looks like it.

– Well then, let's go together.

And so, they walked.
His thermos smelled of raspberries and mint.
Their conversation flowed naturally.
About things hard to explain, and things that didn't need to be named.
Because when you're with someone who doesn't make you try to be interesting – that's the best feeling in the world.

At a turn, between the sparse streetlights, Sakura glanced aside and suddenly said:

– I've always dreamed of climbing that radio tower.

He looked where she pointed.
An old structure in the darkness – with a warning sign, an empty field around it, and stars hanging above.

He nodded.

– Let's fly.

They walked closer. Slipped under the fence.
Began climbing, carefully.
Some steps were missing, their hands slipped, they had to help each other.
Their laughter was quiet. Their breathing – loud.
The fear was real, but so was the joy.

And the tower accepted them.

At the top – only the wind.
Silence.
And a sky that felt closer than ever.

Sakura sat down and froze for a moment.
Below – hundreds of dark meters, a thin platform beneath her feet, a vast emptiness that made her head spin.
And above – an endless dome where stars didn't just sparkle, they breathed.

The wind touched her, and inside, she trembled –
from the height, from awe, from disbelief that
this was real.

The city below scattered its lights.
From up here, it looked like a toy, something
distant and small.
But what was happening between them – was the
most real thing in the world.

– Who are you? – Sakura asked, not taking her
eyes off the stars.

He smiled.

– Just a boy from the train. Or a guide to dreams.
Your choice.

They stayed there a long time.
An hour. Maybe two.
Their words flowed like streams after a thaw.
And then came a silence – warm, welcoming, the
kind that needed nothing more.

When it got truly cold, they began climbing
down.
The descent was scarier. But closer.
Because now they needed no words.
Just a steady hand.
And a glance that said: "I'm here."

They parted at the crossroads.
No names. No promises. No "let's meet again."

Sometimes the most important encounters stay only within you.
Because that's where they can last forever.

Sakura went home late.
But slept like she hadn't in ages – deeply, peacefully, without any worries.

Later, she wouldn't remember his face.
But she would remember how she laughed without a shield.
How she played no role.
How she simply – was.

Maybe he wasn't "her person."
Maybe she just met herself again.
The self she hadn't allowed herself to be in so long – open, silly, brave, light, alive.

Sometimes fate isn't about making you fall in love with someone,
but about making you remember how you can glow – next to someone who simply doesn't dim your light.

Yours, Sakura

Chapter 69. When Friendship Was a Spell

We didn't know it was the last September,
the last tea in the kitchen,
the last walk in the forest –
before everything drifted apart.

Every girl once had friends with whom she became her true self.
Not the girl teachers saw, not the one her mother admired.
But the real one – a little awkward, sometimes loud, but endlessly alive.

For Sakura, they were those friends.
Friends with whom she didn't have to pretend – she simply lived.

They weren't just friends. They were classmates.
The ones she shared a desk with, tugged on each other's sleeves during tests, shared markers and chocolate split three ways.
The ones she grew up with step by step – not by plan, but by heart.
And maybe that's why it was so easy – no need to travel far; they were already there.

Like air. Like the school desk. Like the bell between classes.

School breaks stretched into eternity, and each one mattered more than the lessons.
Letters passed under desks.
Plans for the evening whispered in hushed voices.

In their class, it was as if there were two worlds. One world belonged to the girls who were already grown-up, dating older boys, sneaking off to dark courtyards, pretending they knew everything.
And then there were Sakura and her girls.
They didn't have "boyfriends."
But they had backpacks filled with leaves, a guitar, notebooks with fairy tales, blankets, and forest trails.
They weren't waiting for kisses – they were searching for spells.
They weren't rehearsing adulthood – they were living magic.

Their rituals were real.
They would go into the forest – far from the

houses, where the paths seemed enchanted.
On the slope of a hill, in the soft shade of pine trees, they would spread out a blanket.
That's where the initiations took place.
Each girl would pass through a "magic circle" made of pine cones and string, recite an oath, eat a "sandwich of strength," and become a forest witch.
Then they would sing.
Sakura brought her guitar.
She knew only three chords, but it was enough to sing about everything: the wind, freedom, the kind of friendship no one could break.

They would lie on their backs, staring at the tree canopies.
Laughing until someone screamed because of an ant crawling up their knee.
And then they'd all jump up – loud, awkward, happy.

After school, they would visit each other's homes.
Drinking tea. Dressing up. Trying on their mothers' shoes that were always too big.
Putting on makeup – wildly. Too bright.

Eyeliner trembling, blush in uneven spots.
But it wasn't about makeup – it was about becoming. About courage. About rehearsing womanhood.

They talked about the boys in their class.
Who "definitely looked" at someone in the cafeteria.
Who "seemed to like" a note.
They built strategies. Secret. Smart. Silly. Perfect.
How to walk by, how to laugh, what to do if he suddenly spoke.
But all of it – whispered. In pillows. Over tea mugs.
And always – together.

They believed they would be friends forever.
As if there would always be "at the gate at six," "bring your guitar," "let's meet at the clearing."
As if the adult life, where all this suddenly stops, would never come.

But adult life did come.
One moved away.
Another became a mother.

The third disappeared in endless relocations.
And no one quarreled. No one got upset.
They just – stopped writing. Stopped calling.
Stopped being together.

Sometimes, Sakura tried to find them.
Sometimes. On social media.
Then less often.
Then – she just remembered.

"Hi. I remember how you drew eyes in every notebook.
I remember how you sang with me, as if we really were witches.
I remember how we were a whole universe.
You are an entire era of my heart. But where do I say this? To whom? Why?"

She didn't write.
And maybe she was right.

Because everything important – had already happened.
It didn't need to continue.
It needed to be remembered – gently.

Sometimes the strongest bonds are those that
stay within you,
even when they vanish from the outside.

Sometimes the closest people are the ones you
haven't seen for twenty years,
but you still remember their laughter, the guitar,
tea in the kitchen, and the strategy of "how to
walk past him with your head held high."

They weren't just friends.
They were you. Scattered into parts.
The way you would never be again.
But who still lives within you.
If you close your eyes.

Yours, Sakura

Chapter 70. When Your Place is Taken

Pain isn't a stage you're kicked off.
It's the audience where you sit, pretending you don't care.

When Sakura was in middle school, a new girl joined their class.
Bright. Bold. Far too mature for their age.
She immediately began gathering girls around her, as if she had some special right to do so.
And Sakura – ended up beside her.
Not in the center. But nearby.
She didn't know if they were friends or just happened to share the same space at the same time.
But back then, it felt – important.

One day, the new girl came to class with shining eyes and declared:
– Let's create a dance for the school competition. A real show.

And everything started spinning.
Music. Moves. Rehearsals after school.
Laughter. The sense of something big.

Sakura felt like part of something alive.
She hadn't trained in dance, but inside, she always reached for rhythm, for the feeling of moving,
of flying.

They practiced.
Clumsy. Joyful. Sincere.
There were moments when everything came together.
And moments when nothing worked.
But Sakura went home with that warm feeling inside:
I belong. I exist. I dance.

But then she got sick.
A few days. Then a few more.
And when she returned – the world had shifted slightly.

– We picked another girl, – the new girl said.
– But... you can still be in it. If you want, you can be the fourth.

Sakura walked to the mirror where they rehearsed and saw:
now there were three of them.

They had their own moves. Their own
connection. Their own balance.
The fourth – was extra.
The fourth – was in the background.

– Look, – said another girl, – you can stand here,
at the back… It'll be fine!

But Sakura knew there, at the back, there was no
place for her.
Not by number. By meaning.

She stood by the wall.
Inside, it was like someone was slowly draining
the air from her chest.
Not painful. Just empty.

– I think I won't, – she said.
Calmly. Even gently.
And walked away.

No one called her back.
No one said: "Without you, it's not the same."

She came to the competition.
Sat in the audience, third row.
The music started.
The dance – the one they had created together.

And something inside her tightened,
watching those moves performed by other hands,
moves she remembered as her own.

She didn't know what she felt.
Disappointment? Anger? Jealousy?

No. Not that.

She felt something inside closing,
and something else opening. More mature.

There are stages where you are invited to stand –
but you already feel you are not welcome.
Or you are welcome, but not truly.
Or you are welcome – as long as you agree to be
a shadow.

She left.
And no one noticed.
Or maybe they did.
But they didn't say it.
And that meant more than words.

Some stories never happen.
And you think you missed your chance.
But then, over time, you realize:

it wasn't you who was late.
It simply wasn't yours.

Because what is truly yours –
always lets you be seen.
Not just on a stage. But in someone's heart.

Yours, Sakura

Chapter 71. Those Who Travel Light Are the Ones Who Stay

Sometimes, to return to yourself,
you must first be left with nothing.

Sakura had always known she would end up here one day.
Not because she wanted to. Not because she searched for it.
But because something strange lived inside her –
as if someone was calling her,
not with a voice, but with a direction.

She couldn't explain why she chose this place.
One day, she just stopped resisting.

The flight was smooth. Her belongings were packed.
Everything she needed was with her.
She even smiled – she thought she was ready.
For change. For new encounters. For a new version of herself.

But when the plane landed, her luggage didn't arrive.
The carefully packed suitcase –
filled with her favorite dresses, sleep masks, earrings for every occasion –
simply didn't make it.

And standing there, watching the empty conveyor belt,
Sakura didn't feel panic.
She felt... relief.

At first, she didn't understand why.
But something in her settled – not as despair, but as calm.
As if someone had taken away everything

unnecessary,
leaving only her.

That evening, she bought a dress. Simple.
Sandals. Nothing extra.
And for the first time in her life – she didn't
want to add anything more.

A few days later, they visited a temple.
It wasn't flashy. It didn't call for attention.
It seemed part of the earth itself,
like a stone that owed nothing to anyone.

In the courtyard, on warm stone tiles,
sat a monk in faded orange robes.
He didn't look. He was simply present.
Like a tree.
Like water in a bowl.
Like something that just is.

Sakura slowed her steps.
He nodded slightly.
Not inviting. Not welcoming.
Simply confirming that she had arrived at the
right moment.

She sat beside him.
Not because she knew it was the right thing to do.
But because she felt:
now – no talking.
No explaining.
No pretending.

She closed her eyes.

At first, it was as always.
Thoughts, scattered words, the habit of assessing the moment.
And then – everything suddenly fell away.
Like clothes you take off, not because it's too hot,
but because you no longer need to hide.

There was no revelation.
No voices.
Just space.
Silence.
As if someone turned off the excess light,
leaving only one – soft, from within.

She didn't think, "Now I'm different."
No.

She just felt, for the first time in a long while:
here I am.
Without commentary.
Without the need to justify herself – even to herself.

When she opened her eyes,
everything around her was the same.
But it no longer weighed on her.
The world hadn't become smaller –
she just stopped getting lost in it.

There was a day when everyone wore saris.
The fabric touched her skin gently, almost affectionately,
not decorating her – but accepting her.

Sakura stood by a window, adjusting the folds,
when one of the girls in the group approached.
With a smile, casually, as if in passing,
she handed her a lipstick. Red.

– Such beauty… Especially in this elegant look.
It deserves a highlight.

Sakura took it.
Applied it lightly, in one stroke.

Looked in the mirror.
And for a moment – she stopped.

There, in the reflection, was a face
that no longer tried to please.
No mask. No pretense.

Just her.
The one who no longer hid.
And didn't wait to be approved.

She simply stood by the window –
with an open face and a slightly raised chin.
Like someone who had returned to herself.
Not loudly. Not dramatically.
Just – completely.

And the suitcase?

It came back.
Later. When everything was already over.
When Sakura had returned home,
continued with her life,
and one morning, the courier rang the doorbell.

The suitcase stood on the doorstep – intact,
neatly closed,
just as she had left it.

She opened it.
Everything was there.
Clothes. Toiletries. The perfume bottle she had treasured.
As if nothing had changed.

But she had changed.

She looked at the things,
and understood they were part of an image,
not part of her.
Like a costume you no longer wish to wear,
not because it's tight –
but because it's unnecessary.

She closed the lid.
Without regret.
Without drama.
Simply because she knew:
her suitcase belonged right where it was.
In the past.

And she now walked forward – light as air.

In that journey, she lost many things:
comfort, external control, familiar ways of
keeping herself "together" –

how it was once proper, convenient, acceptable to others.

But that loss allowed her to finally notice:
the scent of air at dawn,
the song of street birds,
the sound of her own breathing,
when nothing else distracted her from the most important thing –
the life within.

She began to listen.
To see.
To live – not from how she appeared,
but from how she felt.

Because too often, we walk with our eyes down,
watching how we are seen,
gathering ourselves, holding our shape –
instead of simply being.

And everything that matters, everything real –
lives above.

To notice it,
you must let go.
And hold on to nothing.

Yours, Sakura

Chapter 72. The Color of a Mistake

Sometimes everything begins with an ordinary afternoon, when you're simply waiting for a friend over tea – and have no idea that, within a few hours, you'll be scrubbing away a whole world that's veered off course.

Two identical brick buildings stood across from each other, separated by a shared courtyard – with swings, cracks in the asphalt, and lilac bushes that bloomed so lavishly in spring that it seemed the earth itself was perfumed.

When the lilacs blossomed, the girls would gather them by the armful, carry them home, and soon the stairwells would be filled with the scent of childhood, sunshine, and school uniforms.

From their balconies, they could see the entire courtyard – and if you shouted from below:
– Hey, come out!
– Just a second! –
…within a few minutes, she would appear – tousled, barefoot, with a candy wrapper in hand and a story forever on her lips.

She was bright. Loud. As if there was a constant music playing within her, one only she could hear.
She loved to boast that she'd soon be signed by a modeling agency. That a photo shoot was almost confirmed.
Of course, it wasn't entirely true. But it wasn't a lie either. Just a dream – one that didn't yet know it had missed its chance.

That weekend, she texted:
"I got a new toner. I'm going to touch up my roots and come over. You'll be the first to see!"

Sunlight poured through the window; tea cooled in the cup.
An hour passed. Then a bit more.

When she finally knocked on the door, everything fell silent.
She stood in the doorway, wearing a hoodie with the hood pulled almost over her eyes. She wasn't laughing. She wasn't chatting.
She simply stepped inside and sank onto the couch. Silent.

When she slowly pulled back the hood, Sakura caught her breath.
Her hair was bright green. Not just green – but vividly, glaringly green.
A color that was hard to call beautiful. And even harder to forgive yourself for.

Her gaze dropped. She clenched her sleeves in her fists.
And in that silence, it wasn't a mistake.
It was vulnerability.

Sakura said nothing. She simply grabbed her bag and ran through the courtyard.
Through the scent of lilacs. Through the patches of sunlight.
To the store.
For black dye. The real kind.

They spent the entire day together.
Dye dripped onto the tiles, foam tickled their wrists, hair tangled in their fingers.
Laughter, splashes, water. Everything returned to black.
Everything became familiar again.

The next day, visiting her friend's kitchen,
Sakura noticed the bottle.
Just a bottle.
She turned it.
And read:
"Malachite."

She hadn't read the label. She'd simply grabbed it – because it looked right.
She thought it was black.
But it was green.

Sometimes we make mistakes not because we crave change, but because we're rushing to save what we love.
We reach for something familiar, thinking: this is it.
But it turns out – it's not. Not at all.

But if there's someone beside you who doesn't laugh,
doesn't say, "It's your own fault,"
but just runs for the dye and stays with you until the water runs clear –

then it's all right.
Even if the balcony rail is draped with a towel

speckled in green.
Even if something inside still stings a little.

Because the most important thing isn't the color.
It's the one who stays beside you until it's washed away.

Yours, Sakura

Chapter 73. 故郷 – furusato – The Homeland of the Soul

They say that if a place greets you in silence,
it means it remembers you.

Sakura arrived in Japan in November –
when the maples blazed with farewell colors,
as though it wasn't the tree losing its leaves,
but the sky burning away the last letters of autumn.

The airport was cool and calm, like the surface of a bowl of rice –

nothing excessive, just the essence.
And the evening train seemed to glide not on tracks, but on memories she hadn't yet lived.

She looked out the window and didn't see a landscape –
but rather turned the pages of an old album,
where the photos had faded,
but the feelings remained.
Familiar traffic lights. Lamps on the station ceiling. The hum of the train.
They weren't new.
They were like a scent from childhood you can't describe,
but immediately recognize.
Like a dream that once seemed so distant it had become air.

People she traveled with would sometimes stop mid-sentence,
glance at her with quiet curiosity, and say:
– You seem different here. Lighter. More authentic.
As if there's a hidden part of you that belongs to this place.
– Look, even your movements have changed.

There's something Japanese in them, subtle, like
a kimono – not a line, but a breath.

She would only nod.
Because she couldn't explain it herself.
But she felt it. Deeply, without words –
as though her soul had finally unfolded its futon
on the floor,
stretched itself out, and breathed: "Home."

In Japan, they say:
the wind knows its tree not by its leaves, but by
the silence with which it welcomes it.
Perhaps a person knows their place not by the
signs,
but by the way it suddenly becomes easy to
breathe there.

She walked along an evening street in Tokyo,
where red leaves danced above the asphalt,
and suddenly she remembered a dream she had
never seen –
but which somehow lingered in her palms, in her
step, in her gaze upon a streetlight.
Sometimes it's not you who remembers, but the
world that remembers you.

And it's not mysticism. It's honesty.
When you find yourself in a place where you
don't have to be better, or happier,
or smarter, or stronger.
You are simply accepted.
Not because you've changed.
But because you've become yourself.

Sometimes a foreign land speaks for us what our
soul has whispered all along –
but we didn't know how to hear.
And sometimes it tells us a truth we were afraid
to admit:
that home is not a place, but an inner
recognition.

Sometimes this recognition comes as déjà vu –
not as a glitch, but as a response.
Not as strangeness, but as a testimony:
you were here. Or you were meant to be.
And now – you are.

Yours, Sakura

Chapter 74. When the Heart Learns to Wait

Sakura never knew how to wait. Waiting felt unbearable to her, like the slow, viscous flow of time that stretches seconds into hours, makes the heartbeat nervously, and forces the mind to find any excuse to leave. But perhaps that is why fate decided to teach her the most unexpected lesson in patience–by connecting her with someone who could never arrive on time.

Their first date began at the exit of the subway station, on a day when the rain poured down as if the sky had decided to shed all its tears at once. Sakura stood beneath a narrow awning, wrapped in a thin scarf, feeling the cold drops still finding their way to her shoulders, sliding off the roof's edge. The passersby flickered like shadows, umbrellas opening and closing, and streams of water flowed along the road, creating a quiet, restless murmur.

The first message came about ten minutes later:

– I'm on my way.

Then another, half an hour after that:

– Sorry, the bus is stuck in traffic. I'm almost there.

Sakura stared at the screen, feeling her patience beginning to fray. She didn't like waiting–she didn't know how to wait. And now it seemed as if the whole world was testing her resolve. She thought of leaving several times, but something held her in place, like a thin, invisible thread connecting her to this person she barely knew yet.

"If I leave now," she thought, "and he asks me out again, I will never be able to trust him. I will never forget this waiting." And that thought, strangely enough, kept her standing there, despite the cold and fatigue.

Twenty more minutes passed. Another notification sounded:

– I'm just one centimeter away, he texted, looking at the map on his phone, where the remaining route appeared so tiny, it seemed like just a single step. Sakura couldn't help but smile.

That "centimeter" on the map turned into almost another hour in real life, and each time she checked the time, her heart clenched again and again with anxiety.

Later she would learn that he had gotten on the wrong bus. In his rush, lost in his thoughts about the meeting, he had accidentally boarded a bus heading in the opposite direction. He realized this only after a few stops, when he looked at the map and saw the small dot slowly drifting away from the meeting place. Panicked, he jumped off at the nearest stop, waited for the right bus, and, clutching his phone to his chest as if it could somehow speed up time, continued his journey to her.

But that wasn't the only time. About a month and a half later, on the day he decided to propose, the story repeated itself. They planned to meet in the morning to spend the day together, but the morning came and went, and he was still nowhere to be seen. Sakura had checked her reflection in the mirror countless times, adjusted her hair, changed her earrings, tried to keep herself busy, but her heart kept returning to one question: "Why isn't he here yet?"

He sent her one message after another:

– Sorry, got held up, something urgent came up.
– Sorry, just a little longer, I need to sort something out.
– Forgive me, but I desperately needed to find some screwdrivers. Special ones.

Sakura read these messages, not understanding what could be so important as to spend half the day searching for screwdrivers. Was he trying to fix something? Was it some crucial tool she knew nothing about? Could it be some kind of super-special screwdriver without which nothing would work?

She smirked, imagining him wandering around shops, examining shelves of tools, while she had been ready for hours.

– Maybe it really is some kind of rare tool, – she murmured, nervously adjusting a strand of her hair.

And it was only when he finally arrived—when she saw him at the doorway, disheveled but with his eyes shining, holding a huge bouquet of red roses—that she realized they were never screwdrivers.

She stepped towards him, her heart froze for a moment, then began to beat so loudly it seemed the whole world should hear it. He knelt down, his hand trembling slightly as he pulled out a small velvet box. And at that moment, a wave of emotion crashed over her so intensely that for a few seconds, her ears felt blocked, like on an airplane. She saw his lips moving, saw the joy glowing in his eyes, but she couldn't hear a word. He was saying something, smiling, and she just stood there, frozen in that moment, not knowing if she was smiling herself or simply paralyzed by shock and surprise.

Only when he fell silent, gazed at her with those bright, smiling eyes, the ring gleaming in his hand—only then did she understand. In that silent, radiant moment, everything she had ever wanted to hear was there. And she realized that all her waiting, all those long hours, had been worth it—

for this look, this smile, this quiet yet infinite happiness.

Her voice slipped out in a whisper, but in that whisper was everything she had ever wanted to say to him:

– Yes. Yes, a thousand times yes.

And only then, when he stood, embraced her, his warm arms wrapping around her, did she realize she was smiling. She felt the happiness slowly spreading through her body, felt her legs weaken slightly, her hands trembling from the rush of emotion. She hugged him tighter, feeling each beat of his heart merging with her own, and whispered, now with confidence:

– Yes. Always.

Sometimes the most important moments in our lives don't arrive in brilliant flashes of joy, but in quiet, patient waiting–when time stretches like a slow spring rain beyond the window. And those who are often late sometimes bring the most unexpected yet most precious gifts into our lives–gifts that change our fate.

Love is not just moments of joy and embraces. It is also the long minutes of waiting, the quiet doubts, the deep faith that something truly important awaits us around every bend in the road. It is the ability to see light even in shadow, to hear the whisper of the heart amid the noise of the world, to find patience where it seemed there was none.

And perhaps those who struggle the most with waiting are the ones who eventually learn to love most deeply–because every moment of their waiting turns into something infinitely precious. Because sometimes the longest roads lead to the brightest moments. And those who arrive, even late, are the ones who stay with us forever.

Yours, Sakura

Chapter 75. When the World Spoke with Her Voice

There are places that don't just make an impression–they awaken something within you. Like an unexpected spring, like a melody heard for the first time, like the first breath after a long winter. The television studio where her adoptive father once took Sakura was one of those places.

At the entrance, they were met by stern security guards. IDs had to be shown; they passed through a metal detector and waited for an escort. Sakura felt the guard's gaze scanning her from head to toe, as if trying to decide if she was worthy of crossing that threshold. But when he saw her standing beside her adoptive father, his expression softened, and he nodded, allowing them through.

The moment they stepped into the main hall, Sakura froze. Around them, people bustled– camera operators with heavy equipment on their shoulders, directors with gleaming tablets, makeup artists carrying cases filled with brushes and glittering eyeshadows. It was like a beehive where everyone knew their place, yet everything moved as a single, living organism. She felt the air was different here–dense, saturated, vibrating like the strings of a guitar before the first chord.

– This is a city within a city, – her father whispered, guiding her towards the elevator. – Here live the true creators–people who don't just work, but craft entire worlds.

When the elevator doors closed, Sakura felt a slight tremor beneath her feet, as if the floor was a living being, breathing alongside them. She closed her eyes, feeling the gentle push as they ascended, feeling the space around them grow tense, like the silence before a play begins, when the audience holds its breath, waiting for the first word.

When the elevator doors opened, they stepped into a long corridor smelling of fresh paint and the faint tang of ozone from the lighting equipment. The air seemed to hum, like the quiet just before a performer steps on stage, before the first lines are spoken, before the brush touches the canvas.

Her adoptive father led her to one of the workshops. Inside, it was quiet, but it was a quiet filled with whispers of ideas, the sound of brushes, the creak of cardboard sheets, and the rustle of sketchbook pages. The air was heavy with the scent of paints, solvents, and old film reels. But the smell wasn't unpleasant—on the contrary, it wrapped around her, pulling her into a state of creative trance.

Sakura paused on the threshold, almost afraid to disturb the magic of this place. The room felt alive, as if the walls themselves were breathing, as if each brushstroke didn't just leave color, but an emotion. On the tables stood models of buildings, scattered pieces of foam board, scraps of cardboard, metallic ribbons glinting under the light, and jars of paint thick as the depths of the sea, clear as morning mist, and bright as the setting sun.

After speaking with the artists, her father led her further, down winding corridors tangled with cables that snaked towards the studios. Finally, they reached a narrow metal staircase leading to a second level. Sakura felt the floor beneath her faintly vibrating from the footsteps, from the energy that filled this place.

– Come, – her father said, gesturing to the stairs.
– I want to show you the heart of every studio.

They climbed the stairs, and Sakura found herself in a narrow room with a glass wall overlooking the studio below. It was like the captain's bridge of a massive ship, from which one could watch everything unfold.

On the walls hung multiple screens, the consoles were covered with buttons and levers, glowing LEDs flickering. The air carried a faint scent of warm electronics and coffee. Through the glass, she saw the host adjusting his jacket, assistants giving final instructions to the cameramen, lighting technicians fine-tuning the spotlights.

One of the sound engineers–a man with short hair and a focused look–noticed her. He nodded slightly and, without taking his eyes off his work, gestured for her to come closer.

Cautiously, she stepped forward, peeking over his shoulder. On his screen, sound waves pulsed, turning human voices into colorful lines.

– See? – he said, still watching the screens. – This isn't just buttons and levers. This is the heart of the studio. Here we turn silence into music, whispers into voices, emotions into sound.

He handed her a pair of large headphones, and Sakura carefully put them on. In that instant, the world around her transformed. She heard the cables creaking, someone whispering into a microphone, the faint creak of the floor beneath an actor's steps. Her heartbeat seemed to sync with this quiet, powerful hum, as if she had become part of this great, living organism.

When the day was nearing its end, her father offered to let her stay for the recording of an evening show. It was a musical program with a guest band, and when the host announced that the audience could ask questions, Sakura felt her heart race. She raised her hand, and when the camera turned towards her, her voice sounded unexpectedly firm:

– Where do you find inspiration for your songs? What do you think about when you play?

The musician smiled, his eyes shining beneath the bright studio lights.

– Sometimes inspiration comes from moments like this, – he said, nodding towards her. – From a glance, from silence, from a chance encounter. Sometimes inspiration is simply the feeling that you are alive, that you can hear the world around you.

The next day, as she was leaving school, one of the boys called out to her:

– Hey, I saw you on TV!

Sakura stopped, turned, and a gentle, slightly shy smile touched her lips. She felt her heart flutter, and she realized that this moment was not just an episode in her life, but the first step into a new, bold, creative reality.

Sometimes, one step, one word, one movement can awaken an entire world within your heart. Sometimes, all it takes is to believe that your voice, your brush, your gaze matters. That each of us is a creator, that each of us can inspire, dream, and shape.

Don't be afraid to leave your mark on this world. Don't be afraid to be yourself. Because perhaps your dreams are the colors that will one day paint an entire universe.

Yours, Sakura

Chapter 76. Epilogue: A Letter to Myself

Sakura had traveled a long road. She had searched for herself in the noise of cities, in the whisper of forests, in the reflections of sunsets over warm seas. She had learned not to fear waiting, to forgive, to let go, and to begin again. She had learned to hear the silence and speak with her own voice, to find her place among endless roads and to lose herself–only to find herself again.

She realized that life is not just a sequence of points, but a dance between light and shadow, between words and silence, between beginnings and endings. That each moment is a letter we write to ourselves, sometimes without even realizing that these lines will stay with us forever.

And if these lines have reached you, it means there is a place in your heart for silence, for questions, for brave dreams. Perhaps, sometimes you feel lost, perhaps your voice seems too quiet, your dreams too distant. But know this–

with in you is an entire universe, full of unfinished melodies, unsent letters, and unspoken words. Do not be afraid to be yourself, do not fear making mistakes, do not fear of being heard. For in every step you take, in every glance, in every breath, there is that very light that never fades, even when darkness seems to surround you.

So go on. Write your own letter. Fill your life with colors, sounds, and words. Create, dream, love. And remember that your heart continues to bloom, like an eternal Sakura, even in the coldest days.

With love,
Sakura.